OSCAR ESCALLADA ALLENDE

YOU WERE BORN HAPPY!

100 REASONS FOR LIVING AND NOT DYING

1,000 THOUGHTS, FEELINGS AND ACTIONS TO BE HAPPY ALL THE TIME

TAG Publishing, LLC
2030 S. Milam
Amarillo, TX 79109
www.TAGPublishers.com
Office (806) 373-0114
Fax (806) 373-4004
info@TAGPublishers.com

ISBN: 978-1-59930-412-0

First Edition

Copyright © 2012 Oscar Escallada Allende

All rights reserved. No part of this book may be reproduced in any form without prior written permission from the publisher. The opinions and conclusions drawn in this book are solely those of the author. The author and the publisher bear no liability in connection with the use of the ideas presented.

Quantity discounts are available on bulk orders.
Contact info@TAGPublishers.com for more information.

OSCAR ESCALLADA ALLENDE

YOU WERE BORN HAPPY!

100 REASONS FOR LIVING AND NOT DYING

1,000 THOUGHTS, FEELINGS AND ACTIONS TO BE HAPPY ALL THE TIME

You Were Born Happy!

ACKNOWLEDGMENTS

This work is mainly dedicated to all the men and women who ever had the hope of improving their lives and had the courage to follow their heart´s desires.

To my mom, Milagros Allende, for teaching me the real meaning of unconditional love, every day.

To my dad, Jose Luis Escallada, for making me realize from a very early age my unlimited potential and that dreams do come true.

To my parents, this book is for you. My deepest gratitude for two of the most valuable gifts a son could ever wish for, unconditional love and the desire to go after one´s dreams. These are the rocking stones upon which I have built, I am building and will always build my life.

To my wonderful grandmothers, may they rest in peace. They saw a special gift in me before I even realized. As time went by, the gift flourished and it has become reality in the form of a wonderful book today. I am sure your souls are smiling. I send you the wisdom of this writing with all my love.

To my brother, Chelis, and my two sisters, Yolanda and Laura. Thank you for teaching me the important lessons in life.

To my soul mate, Carolina Resendiz, who loves me, supports me every step of the way and cheers me up when I am down.

To all my friends and work colleagues. May the words in this book help you with the numerous challenges of daily life.

To all my followers on www.happyglobe-oe.com This is for you all.

God bless you.

You Were Born Happy!

CONTENTS

Foreword by Bob Proctor..........9
The Lost 10 Secrets of Happiness..........12
The Beginning of the Search..........19
INTRODUCTION..........21

FIRST PART THE AGES OF HAPPINESS

1. The child. You were born happy..........28
2. The adult. The lord of the kingdoms..........32
3. The old. The wisdom of the ages..........35

SECOND PART

1. Thoughts..........55
2. Feelings..........70
3. Actions..........85
4. Individual being..........99
5. Social being..........114
6. Health..........129
7. Having..........144
8. Profession..........159
9. Finances..........173
10. Spirituality..........188

THIRD PART PRACTICE OF HAPPINESS

1. Daily practice..........205
2. The power of the mind..........209
3. Emotional and social intelligence..........210
4. How can I be happier?..........212
Start creating miracles in your life!..........214

CONCLUSION

Conclusion..........217
Author: Oscar Escallada..........220
Happy Globe..........221
Happiness Coaching Program..........223

You Were Born Happy!

FOREWORD

Many of the greatest philosophers and brilliant minds knew the secret to a successful and happy life. They were the greatest people in history: Plato, Shakespeare, Newton, Lincoln, Emerson, Edison and Einstein among others. I have spent most of my adult life studying people – why we do the things we do and don't do some of the things we should. Now Oscar Escallada is exposing the secret of success and happiness in an accessible and straightforward way that every person can understand and apply to their lives.

Always grateful for what he had and the core values that were instilled in him which have served him well over the years, Oscar had an innate awareness that there was more in store for him from a very young age. His experience of coming from a modest background to achieve the pinnacle of success both professionally and personally is an inspiring read. He teaches the very same principles he has experienced to lead a more fulfilled life.

We each have the power to choose each day how we will live and what our results will be; this concept is foreign to most people. It all begins in the mind. Change your mental focus and you will change your life. Your thoughts create mental images, images create feelings, feelings produce certain winning actions, which in return, produce wonderful results in all areas of your life. In addition to comprehensive information and numerous stories, Oscar has the talent and a compelling style to make these wonderful lessons easy to grasp.

Napoleon Hill's classic *Think and Grow Rich* has perhaps transformed more lives and created more riches than any other book available today. Since its introduction in 1937, millions of copies have been sold around the world. It still remains one of the top-selling books of its kind. This book, *You Were Born Happy*, is founded on exactly those principles and the principles in *You Were Born Rich*.

For more than four decades I've dedicated my life to the study of human potential.

I have experienced circumstances similar to Oscar's in my own life and used these same concepts to create an entirely new reality. *You Were Born Happy* can be your first step forward to a better life. By understanding why you are getting certain results in life, you glean the awareness of what is needed to move forward and for many people it is a welcomed and life changing event.

As you travel through its pages and you learn the secrets to happy living, you will come to know how you can have, be, or do anything you want. You will realize that you have all the resources within you to have an extraordinary and happy life. Decide and commit right now to live a life that is worthy of you. Your life will never be the same again.

**Bob Proctor, Teacher in The Secret
and bestselling author of *You Were Born Rich***

THE LOST 10 SECRETS OF HAPPINESS!

1. YOUR GREATEST TREASURE
THE POWER OF YOUR MIND

Increase your confidence, find out what you want, create different options, overcome obstacles, produce the results you want and gain the wisdom of success.

2. THE SECRET TO HAPPINESS
INCREASE POSITIVE EMOTIONS & ELIMINATE NEGATIVE FEELINGS

Past. Focus on the positive, learn and move on.
Present. What positive emotions do you want? Learn to feel them!
Future. Hope, optimism and action are your best friends.

3. THE BIGGEST ACHIEVEMENT OF THE HUMAN RACE FREEDOM OF ACTION.

Find a powerful WHY and you will unleash your unlimited power.
What would you do if you could not fail?
Become an expert in giving meaning to your life.

4. YOUR PERSONAL CODE OF EXCELLENCE.

How would you like to be in all areas of life: thinking, feeling, actions, your individual virtues, social relationships, health, possessions, profession, wealth and spiritual experience?

5. YOU CHOOSE YOUR LIFE!
CONQUERING HUMAN RELATIONSHIPS

You choose what relationship you want to have with yourself, as a son/daughter, brother/sister, friend, lover, at work, in your community, as a parent, grandparent and with the world.

THE LOST 10 SECRETS OF HAPPINESS!

6. HEALTH = THE WISDOM OF A BALANCED LIFE
Take immediate control of your mind & body harmony, develop emotional intelligence, have a spectacular body, improve your social relationships and be your best at work.

7. YOU CAN HAVE IT ALL!
From lack of awareness to extraordinary results, from average performance to success and excellence, and from poverty and emptiness to wealth and meaning of life.

8. WHAT DO YOU WANT TO DO FOR A LIVING? ANYTHING IS POSSIBLE!
Go from routine and boredom to realization in your dream profession through a well-planned transition. Master the art of human relations and leadership. Show your gift to the world!

9. HOW MUCH MONEY DO YOU WANT? WHAT ARE YOU WILLING TO DO FOR IT?
Go from confusion to absolute clarity, from lack of ability to expert and from a meaningless existence to leaving your legacy.

10. DEVELOPING YOUR SPIRITUAL BEING!
First, become a helper to those around you.
Second, develop and enjoy your spiritual connection.
Last, learn as much as you can and let wisdom be your guiding principle in life.

You Were Born Happy!

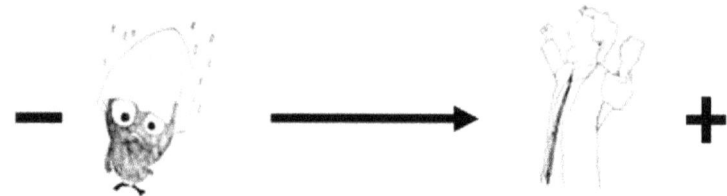

THOUGHTS
1. Low Self-esteem - Winner's Image
2. Low Confidence - High Confidence
3. Confusion - Clarity
4. Indecisiveness - Power of Decision
5. Indifference - Commitment
6. Lack of Faith - Belief
7. Boredom - Enthusiasm
8. Inefficiency - Efficiency
9. Under achievement - Results
10. Ignorance - Wisdom

FEELINGS
11. Regret - Pride
12. Blindness - Gratitude
13. Sadness - Joy of Life
14. Unhappiness - Happiness
15. Lack of Affection - Love
16. Selfishness - Contribution
17. Hesitation - Determination
18. Passivity - Passion
19. Worry - Hope
20. Pessimism - Optimism

ACTIONS
21. Unawareness - Unlimited Power
22. Emotional Ignorance - Emotional Intelligence
23. Paralysis - Total Motivation
24. Procrastination - Personal Virtues
25. Poor Relations - Fulfilling Relationships

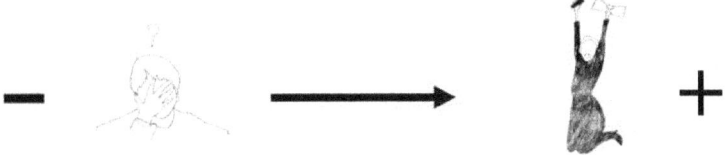

26.	Health Problems	-	Long Healthy Life
27.	Mediocrity	-	Excellence
28.	Average Performance	-	Constant Improvement at Work
29.	Wealth Student	-	Expert
30.	Emptiness	-	Meaning of Life

INDIVIDUAL BEING

31.	Chaos	-	Order
32.	Lack of control	-	Self-control
33.	Laziness	-	Determination
34.	Immaturity	-	Maturity
35.	Lack of Engagement	-	Responsibility & Leadership
36.	Excess	-	Moderation
37.	Irregular Effort	-	Persistence
38.	Apathy	-	Hard Work
39.	Lack of Control	-	Financial Independence
40.	Lack of Faith	-	Religion & Spirituality

SOCIAL BEING

41.	Unawareness	-	Self-knowledge
42.	Unfulfilling Relations	-	Children´s Love
43.	Family Conflicts	-	Understand Brothers & Sisters
44.	Resentment	-	Loyalty between Friends
45.	Conditioned Love	-	Unconditional Love
46.	Average Performance	-	Your Best All the Time
47.	Lack of Concern	-	Responsibility as Social Leader
48.	Neglect	-	Care
49.	Inexperience	-	Wisdom
50.	Individuality	-	Oneness with humanity

You Were Born Happy!

HEALTH

51.	Weakness	-	Mental Hygiene
52.	Distress	-	Mind-Body Harmony
53.	Unconsciousness	-	Emotional Proficiency
54.	Lack of Control	-	Stability of Character
55.	Unhealthy Body	-	Spectacular Body
56.	Disease	-	Health
57.	Broken Families	-	Happy Families
58.	Loneliness	-	Joy of Human Relations
59.	Unbalanced Life	-	Family & Work
60.	Being Lost	-	Healthy Ambition

POSSESSIONS & HAVING

61.	Ignorance	-	Powerful Mind
62.	Emotional Poverty	-	Emotional Wealth
63.	Poor Results	-	Extraordinary Results
64.	Mediocrity	-	Full Potential
65.	Limitations	-	Abundance Awareness
66.	Addictions	-	Healthy Leisure Time
67.	Failure	-	Success
68.	Low Performance	-	Excellence
69.	Scarcity	-	Amazing Wealth
70.	Emptiness	-	Life's Purpose

PROFESSION

71.	Frustration	-	Dream Profession
72.	Routine	-	Happiness at Work
73.	Lack of Planning	-	Job-Hunt Plan
74.	Burn-Out Syndrome	-	Constant Development
75.	Difficult Relations	-	Negotiation Expert

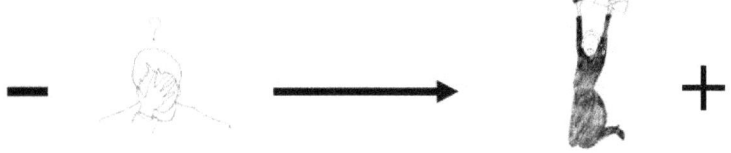

76.	Employee	-	Businessman
77.	Lack of Strategy	-	War Tactics
78.	Individuality	-	Team Work
79.	Low Pay	-	One Million Dollars
80.	Employee	-	Millionaire

FINANCES

81.	Indetermination	-	Clarity
82.	Insecurity	-	Power
83.	Labyrinth	-	Focus & Action Plan
84.	Worm	-	Butterfly
85.	Limited Horizons	-	World View
86.	Reality	-	Dreams
87.	Poverty	-	Real Wealth
88.	Weakness	-	Strength
89.	Poor Mentality	-	Rich Mentality
90.	Ignorance	-	Riches

SPIRITUALITY

91.	Ignorance	-	Knowledge
92.	Theory	-	Practice
93.	Wishing	-	Daily Actions
94.	Powerlessness	-	Daily Miracles
95.	Selfishness	-	Social Responsibility
96.	Vulnerability	-	Happiness
97.	Fragility	-	Strength in Happiness
98.	Doubt	-	Spirituality at Work
99.	Unbalance	-	Balanced Life
100.	Ignorance	-	Wisdom of Happiness

THE BEGINNING OF THE SEARCH

As wise men say, the most difficult step of any endeavor is the first step. Let us now take the first step together. As in the picture, you are that man looking over the large landscape before him. The mountains, rivers and blue sky have been there for millions of years. Do you know what they are asking him? They are whispering: "What are you going to do with your life? What are you going to do with all the minutes that were given to you? There is only one lifetime, make the most out of it!"

Dear reader, I invite you to take such advice and make your life worthwhile living. First, dream without limit. Second, choose the three most important dreams. Third, make a daily plan and follow it with discipline and determination. Four, develop knowledge of your spiritual being, because this will give you strength and help you make the right decisions when the going gets tough. Five, reward yourself as much as you can for your success and be grateful for the journey you are taking. Finally, never give up. The only failure is giving up, the rest is just results, you learn and move on.

Many years ago I read that the greatest artists of all time mentioned they were just mere mediums of their work, just co creators of an unexplainable inspiration. Now, I think I understand. I feel the same way. I do not know why I have had such a strong calling and desire to write a book about happiness for many years. I do not know where the ideas for the structure of the book come from and how to write it. What I do is relax, have a pretty general idea of the message I want to convey and let God do the rest.

My humble aim is twofold. On the one hand, I would like my work to be an inspiration of hope for every single person on this planet who ever wondered how to lead a happier life. On the other hand, I would like to make my contribution to humanity explaining the essence of happiness and making people realize that we are all the same, we all want to lead a happier, wealthier and healthier life. I would also like the reader to follow the worldwide movement we created on www.happyglobe-oe.com, where the main goal is to share happiness with the world.

The greatest secret to happiness is what you focus your mind on every single second of your life. Learn to direct such focus and your life will miraculously be transformed. Remember, to be happy, you just have to allow yourself to be happy in the present NOW. The antidote for unhappiness is the following:

• **The past**. Leave the past where it belongs. Focus on the positive memories and lessons and move on.

• **The present**. Allow yourself to be happy now all the time. Be aware of all your blessings, the marvelous harmonious machinery of your body, the power of your mind, the amazing world of emotions and the joy of being alive, of enjoying nature, enjoying doing something you like, enjoy receiving and giving love and learn to develop the peace of mind the spiritual connection provides.

• **The future**. Always have some dreams, some worthy projects, something to hope for. This will help you overcome the inevitable obstacles of daily life.

INTRODUCTION

Dear reader,

I encourage you start a new adventure with me. Let us make the most out of the days, hours and minutes we were given on this earth, creating a more satisfying, enriching and happier life.

My name is Oscar Escallada, I have just turned 40 years of age, I am Spanish from a beautiful city in the north of Spain called Santander. From a very early age I was most passionate about books, knowledge, adventure, success and happiness. I have had my share of success and failure in different areas of my life, just like everyone else. My academic education includes two bachelor degrees (psychology and conference interpreter) and three master's degrees (hotel management, human resources and business administration).

I have spent half my life traveling, working and studying in different countries (United States, Canada, United Kingdom, Germany, France, Mexico and Cuba). Nowadays I work in Cuba as a general hotel manager for an important, worldwide Spanish hotel company.

Why this book now?

Positive psychology is my passion. This is the science of maximizing satisfaction levels in one's own life, as opposed to the traditional psychology, focused on clinical problems like depression, anxiety and numerous internal conflicts.

I have read more than 500 books on happiness, success, relationships and many areas of life and it is my moment to express to the world that there is hope, life is a marvelous adventure and reality is just a very personal and subjective interpretation of what the majority of people call existence.

Why is this work different from the rest?

There are tons of books and programs in the market about happiness. However, every time I read a book I always have the same two challenges, I cannot remember half of it and the remaining half of it, I just do not know how to apply it to my life on a daily basis.

This book is a treasure map that will take you to a whole new journey of discovery. You will discover the three ages of happiness, the ten kingdoms where the treasures of happiness are hiding and the lost art of applying the science of happiness to your life immediately. You and I, together, will get rid of the darkness of the past, focus and enjoy the present to the maximum and envision and create the future of your dreams.

Le us get started. Your world will never be the same again.

What is my secret?

My secret is that of the ancient Greek philosophers and the great scientists of modern psychology: "Reality does not exist," it is just mere interpretation based on our beliefs, dreams, moods and hopes. My happiness formula is mainly a constant focus on gratitude, inspired actions towards your dreams and love towards your fellow human beings as often as you possibly can.

How can YOU apply it to YOUR life?

It is easy if you know how: focus your thoughts, feelings and actions in everything you desire and it will manifest in your life. You and I, all of us, have a genie inside ourselves. We only have to trust that internal force, focus on all our dreams, persist and, in the majority of cases, your dreams will become reality sooner than you ever thought possible.

How can YOU lead a happy life?

> 1. **Find out what you really want.** If you are not very sure, do some research, ask, experiment and, above all, listen to yourself. I am sure you will find it. What you are looking for is looking for you in return. Imagine life like a large department store where you can get everything you want. You only have to ask for it.

2. **Thank God or the universe** for every positive and good thing you enjoy in your life twice a day, as you get up in the morning and as you go to bed at night. Feel, think, imagine and act as though your dreams have already come true. Those feelings of security, excitement and gratitude are your most precious jewels! These are the treasures that will make you have passion and vision. They will be your best friends in times of storm, when your strength is at its lowest point.

3. **Have a long-run plan** (10-20 years) and a short-run plan (5-1 years). The rest is just a matter of doing steadily but surely and enjoying the process. You can leave the past where it is. If you can learn something from past experiences, do so; if not, you have your dreams to go to, enjoying every second.

4. **Help others in all you can.** Whenever you have all the things you desire (the houses, the cars, the relationships, travels, etc…), what else will you want? Whenever we do something for someone with no selfish interest, we enjoy a very special state of gratitude, satisfaction and happiness that very few other experiences can match.

5. **Be an example of love.** Love yourself first, love your soul mate, your children, your parents, your friends, your work mates, your neighbors, your pet, your community, your nation and mother earth. You will be blessed every step of the way.

Why is this book different?

It is absolutely practical. You will be able to discover a treasure (powerful human values) in each chapter. By the end of the book you will have a new set of tools to take your life to a whole new level. You will be a different person with 1,000 new thoughts, feelings and actions to be happier in all areas of your life (mental, physical, emotional, professional, financial, social and spiritual).

The key to constant happiness is mind focus. Let me explain two different ways of understanding life with an analogy of a garden. The dirty and untidy backyard garden represents the confused mind, with no clear goals, full of fears and insecurities.

On the contrary, a well looked-after, clean and tidy garden represents a perfectly well organized mind, focused on the beautiful side of life, rejecting everything that causes unhappiness and suffering.

Before we enter the different kingdoms to find the treasures, let me ask you a couple of questions. Meditate on them and look for the answers during your journey through the ten kingdoms. Let us dream together:

1. First of all, relax in your favorite room of the house.

2. Imagine you are talking to the genie of the lamp.

3. Realize that the worst thing that can happen to anyone of us is to reach old age with a feeling of regret. Regret for not having been brave enough to take massive action towards the realization of your dream. On the other hand, you will be blessed at the end of your days, when you can say: "I did all I could with what I had. I tried with all my heart. Fear never won the battle. "

4. Imagine yourself at age 90, sitting in a rocking chair on the porch of your home, enjoying a summer sunset and evaluating your life – successes and failures, joys and sorrows, ups and downs and that whole adventure called life. Ask yourself: "If I could be born again, what would I do different? If I knew, I could not fail, what would I dedicate every minute of my waking hours to? You know what?"

"Life is a theatre play where you can not rehearse... So, sing, laugh, dance, cry and live with passion every minute of your life before the curtain closes and the play finishes with no applause."
-Charles Chaplin

YOU DO NOT HAVE TO REACH AGE 90!!!

CREATE THE LIFE OF YOUR DREAMS IN YOUR MIND RIGHT NOW AND MANIFEST IT IN THE PHYSICAL WORLD.

PLEASE, IT IS OF VITAL IMPORTANCE THAT YOU ANSWER THESE QUESTIONS.

1. What kind of thinking do you want to have?

2. What feelings do you long for?

3. What actions do you want to take?

4. Who do you want to be?

5. What social relations would you love to develop?

6. What physical body and wellbeing would you love?

7. What are your dream possessions (cars, houses…)?

8. What is your dream profession?

9. How much money do you want?

10. What kind of spiritual existence do you desire?

CONFUSION

LET US GO TOGETHER FROM CONFUSION TO ORDER, FROM THE NEGATIVE TO THE POSITIVE SIDE OF ALL 100 HUMAN VALUES

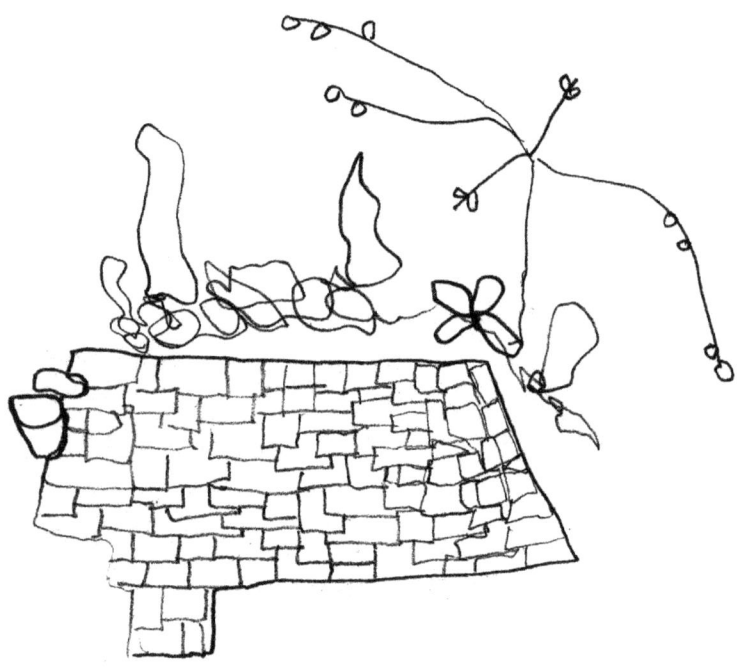

ORDER

FIRST PART: THE AGES OF HAPPINESS

1. THE CHILD. YOU WERE BORN HAPPY.

Child: Mom, dad, I want to be happy!

Mom: Dear son, are you not happy?

Child: Well, yes, sometimes, not all the time.

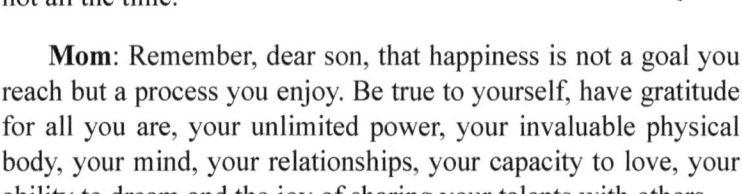

Mom: Remember, dear son, that happiness is not a goal you reach but a process you enjoy. Be true to yourself, have gratitude for all you are, your unlimited power, your invaluable physical body, your mind, your relationships, your capacity to love, your ability to dream and the joy of sharing your talents with others.

1. Child: Sometimes I get confused!

Dad: Do not worry, that happens to everybody once in a while! Ask yourself what you truly want, believe in yourself, form a mental picture of your desires, take daily actions towards your dreams and clarity will appear.

2. Child: Why do I feel sad sometimes?

Mom: Feeling sad is a temporary state. It normally happens because we don´t get something we want. Look for the cause and you will solve it. And don´t forget to focus on gratitude, forgiveness and kindness.

3. Child: What can I do to be happy?

Dad: Listen to your heart´s desire, have faith in yourself and take massive action every day. You will be happy as surely as night follows day.

4. Child: I want to be popular like Peter!

Mom: If you want to be loved, love everybody unconditionally. First, search for your talents and abilities and help everybody you can and you will also be loved by everyone.

5. **Child: How do I solve a problem with a friend?**

Dad: Sometimes we want to be right and we don't listen to other people. Be kind, love them, listen with compassion and help them. They will love you in return.

6. **Child: I feel tired all the time!**

Mom: First, you have to be passionate about life, try to enjoy every minute, regardless of what you are doing. Second, take care of your body and your body will take care of you. Give it good food, lots of rest and exercise.

7. **Child: I want to have everything I desire!**

Dad: And you will. I haven't got the slightest doubt. Focus on your dreams, take daily action, don't harm anybody, help others on the way as much as you can and the universe will provide you with the rest.

8. **Child: John, my best friend, knows exactly what he wants to do when he grows up. How can I find out?**

Mom: Imagine your are at your own funeral, seeing all the people who went to visit you for the last time. What would you like them to say about you. And more important, what would you like your last thought to be? A thought that summarizes your life and fills your heart with pride and satisfaction and brings a peaceful smile to your face? That is your purpose in life!

9. **Child: I want to be rich!**

Dad: Ok, son. Write down the specific amount, date and the service you are willing to provide to society, take massive action, develop discipline and persistence, and it will be yours.

10. **Child: Do you believe in God?**

Mom: I believe in universal laws, I believe we all have a spiritual side and I believe in the goodness of human beings. But, that is something you can only answer for yourself.

SUMMERY OF WHY ALL HUMAN BEINGS ARE BORN HAPPY

You know, happiness is important! Happy children learn better, happy employees perform better at work, even happy cows produce milk of better quality. Politicians and economists have realized that the wealthiest nations are not necessarily the happiest. The most important thing in life is feeling happy with one's life.

In reality being happy is a gift. A gift to yourself first, a gift to your family, a gift to all people you come in contact with and a gift to society.

For some strange reason we always find excuses for not allowing ourselves to be happy in the present, but later and that future never comes! "I will be happy when…" seems to be an unwritten rule in society. You do not need to wait for anything to happen. Be happy now and that will bring more happiness in the future! Otherwise, when are you going to be happy? When you start university or when you finish university and you get your first job? When you buy the car? When you have a girlfriend or a boyfriend? When you buy the house? When you have children? When your children leave the home? When you retire? So please, be happy now.

Let us do an exercise together, right now, and I will show you that you do not need anything to feel fulfilled, to have peace of mind and feel a sense of oneness with the universe.

Nothing and no one will ever make you happy in a million years! You are the center of your universe, you and only you will make yourself happy, not this book, not other courses. Remember, put in your mind what you want to see in your world. Make a choice to be happy. You do not have to do anything to be happy. Put yourself first, do not put happiness at the end of a long to-do list.

Relax, put on relaxing music and do not be disturbed, take a deep breath. Just allow yourself to be happy, no pretense, not trying, just be… do nothing and be happy, do not resist anything, just notice the wonderful sensations of peace and oneness with the universe, give up resistance to any stereotypes and just allow it. You were born happy, forget all objections, there is no, "I want to be happy but..." Forget the "buts," release tension; this is the best moment of your day, the best day of your life, your gift to God.

You do not have to be perfect, enjoy being just you. Happiness is a lightness of being, it is giving up all resistance. Make the decision to stay in the present now, forget the past and the future. Now, the time is now. Say yes to happiness all the time. Be free. Forgive and forget. You do not need a reason. Happiness is a normal state of being. Happy for no reason; that is your new motto. Do not spend your life going to be happy... just be it.

Three other elements that can help you increase your level of fulfillment in the present time. They are: your conception of life in general, of the past and of the future.

As we mentioned before, what is perception and reality? The good news is that you are the ruler of your mind, you decide what things mean to you. Focus on the positive and only expect the best in your life and that is exactly what you will experience.

Regarding the past, we all have lessons to learn and negative experiences, that is the process of growing. Learn from the baby. It falls a thousand times before it manages the art of walking. Have you seen a baby complaining about the process of walking?

As for the future, please, have dreams, big or small, you become an interesting person when you are interested in life. The bigger and stronger your desire for something, the bigger your strength will be when the going gets tough.

2. THE ADULT

THE TEN KINGDOMS OF HAPPINESS

In the child we realized that everyone is born in a natural state of happiness. It is the search for more happiness that makes us unhappy, paradox as it sounds.

I would like the reader to see this book as a very personal search. I would also like the reader to imagine himself/herself on a quest. Imagine a map of happiness. In order to reach total happiness the searcher will have to go through all 10 kingdoms (10 areas of life). In each kingdom there are 10 treasures (the positive side of each human value) and 100 jewels in each area of life (100 thoughts, feelings and actions) to be found. At the end of the quest, dear reader, you will have 1,000 tools to focus your mind, your heart and your actions on to be able to lead an extraordinary, happy and fulfilled life.

You were born happy is all there is to know to lead a happy life. It may sound too simple, but do not let such simplicity deceive you. Simple does not mean easy. For example, we all know that a healthy diet consists mainly of fruit, vegetables, vitamins and water. It is simple, but not many people find it easy to avoid eating junk food and following a nutritious and healthy diet.

The key to happiness is awareness. We have all been programmed in a certain way since we were born, going through childhood, school, some people university, working life and most people carry such ideas about life to the grave.

You know, we all have a genie inside of us, in our mind, in our spirit. It is there for you, waiting for you to tell him what you want and need. The genie says: "Dear Master, believe in yourself, believe in me. Together we can accomplish any task we set our minds to. Ask and it will be granted."

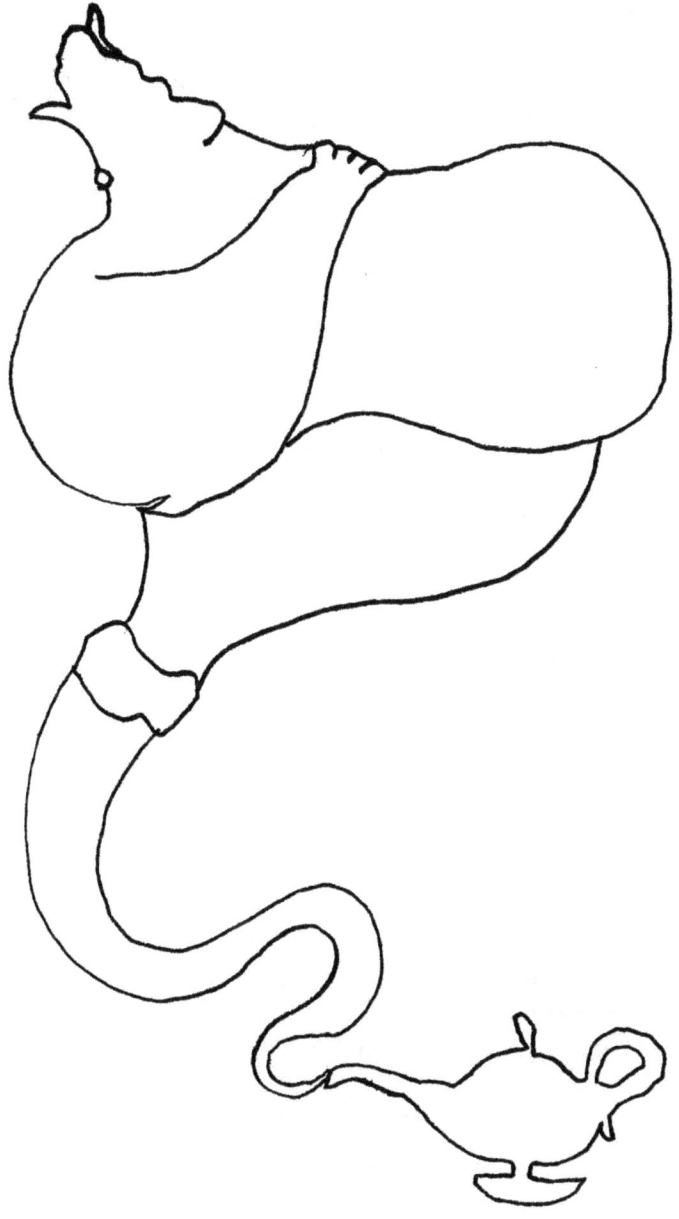

MEET THE GODS AND YOUR IDEAL LIFE

Dear reader, you are not alone! As Alfred Einstein said: "Imagination is much more important than knowledge." This means that you can use one of your mental faculties (imagination) to support you in whatever you desire. Many years ago I read that when you feel alone or confused, you can always sit, relax in a quiet place and ask your favorite personalities (politicians, famous actors, singers, philosophers, etc…), dead or alive, whatever it is that troubles you. It has worked for me in many situations, when I needed wisdom.

You see, we are going to go through ten kingdoms and in each kingdom a god or a goddess will be by our side in case we need them. I encourage you to make the most out of their help, as they possess all the wisdom of the ages. May I introduce to you our life experts in the ten areas of life. Ask them for advice and follow it, you will not regret it:

1. God Jupiter. King of the gods and ruler of Mount Olympus, god of the sky and thunder.
2. Goddess Juno. Queen of the gods and the goddess of marriage, family and love.
3. God Neptune. Lord of the seas, earthquakes and horses.
4. God Vulcan. Master blacksmith and craftsman of the gods, God of fire and the forge.
5. Goddess Vesta. Goddess of the hearth and of the right ordering, of domesticity and the family.
6. Goddess Hygiene. Queen of health.
7. God Pluto. King of riches and good fortune.
8. God Mercury. Master of trade, profit and commerce.
9. Goddess Abundia. Goddess of success, prosperity, abundance, good fortune and protector of savings, investments and wealth.
10. Goddess Minerva. Queen of wisdom and spiritual experience.

3. THE OLD - THE WISDOM OF THE AGES

Dear reader, realize, please, one thing. You can be, do and have anything and everything you want!

Reality does not exist and we are all beings with infinite potential. Make your life an extraordinary adventure!

In this part I would like to make a brief explanation of crucial and important subjects to give you a sense of relativity. Everything and anything as such does not have much meaning. Meaning is created by comparison.

Always remember: Whenever you are faced with a difficult and challenging situation, compare to the concepts below and I assure you, that you will gain strength to carry on.

The main idea is to put life in its true perspective and make you realize the spiritual side of life and how relative everything is, our fears, obstacles and insecurities.

1. The earth in the universe.

2. The evolution of the human race.

3. The mystery of life: from birth to death.

4. The mystery of God.

5. The secret to life: law of attraction.

6. What is reality? A perception issue.

7. Unlimited power of the human being.

8. What is fear and how to handle it?

9. What would you do if you could not fail and you had all the money and resources in the world?

10. How many minutes do you have left and what are you going to do about it?

1. The earth in the universe

For many centuries, our ancestors thought the Earth was the center of the universe. Now, science lets us know that our ancestors were incredibly bad guessers. The Earth is located in the Orion Spur off the Perseus Arm in the Milky Way galaxy. Just where the Milky Way galaxy falls in the scope of the entire universe is still to be determined.

The Milky Way galaxy alone is estimated to measure 1,000 light years from side to side. If the Milky Way were an ocean, the Earth would not even be as large as a drop of water. But how large is the universe?

This we do not know, because we only can estimate the size of the observable universe, which has a diameter 280 billion light years across.

We live on one of those tiny pieces of land for a short period of time. Do you think it is worth worrying about things? We are born with nothing and we are going to be buried with nothing, we cannot take anything with us. The only thing we can do while on earth is to take care of our bodies, love ourselves, our loved ones and the rest of the universe, enjoy life to the fullest (very personal perception) and try to leave the world a bit better than we found it.

It is all a matter of right thinking. The sages of the centuries have united in telling us that, "As a man thinketh in his heart, so is he." The law is always the same. The quality of your thoughts determines the quality of your emotions.

Positive or negative emotions produce a corresponding positive or negative vibration, which in turn attracts positive or negative experiences. Let us choose positive and healthy thoughts to create positive emotions.

We will produce positive vibrations, constructive actions and positive results in our lives. Try it! It has always worked and it always will. It is the law of Universe.

2. The evolution of the human race

The modern theory concerning the evolution of man proposes that humans and apes derive from an apelike ancestor that lived on earth a few million years ago. The theory states that man, through a combination of environmental and genetic factors, emerged as a species to produce the variety of ethnicities seen today, while modern apes evolved on a separate evolutionary pathway.

In the early Pleistocene, 1.5–1 Ma, in Africa, Asia, and Europe, some populations of Homo habilis are thought to have evolved larger brains and made more elaborate stone tools; these differences and others are sufficient for anthropologists to classify them as a new species, Homo erectus. In addition, Homo erectus was the first human ancestor to walk truly upright. This was made possible by the evolution of locking knees and a different location of the foramen (the hole in the skull where the spine enters). They may have used fire to cook their meat.

As you see, our ancestors (homo ergaster, antecessor, erectus, rhodesiensis, neanderthalensis) have been around for the last two million years and the modern homo sapiens have been on earth 250,000 years. If a person's living expectancy nowadays is 80 years, in relation to 2 million years, that makes a tiny 0.004% of our existence. It looks insignificant, does it not?

Besides, if we compare the age of the earth (4,500 million years) with the age of the human being (2 million years) that makes 0.04%, we have not even been around for 1% of the total amount of time.

Have you also realized we live on a huge ball of fire spinning on itself? To a universal traveler, Earth may seem to be a harmless little planet in the far reaches of one of billions of spiral galaxies in the universe.

Earth began to form over 4.5 billion years ago from the same cloud of gas (mostly hydrogen and helium) and interstellar dust that formed our sun, the rest of the solar system and even our galaxy.

By 3.8 to 4.1 billion years ago, Earth had become a planet with an atmosphere (not like our atmosphere today!) and an ocean. About 4.1 billion years ago, the Earth's surface -- or crust -- began to cool and stabilize, creating the solid surface with its rocky terrain.

For the next 1.3 billion years (3.8 to 2.5 billion years ago), called the Archean Period, **first life** began to appear (at least as far as our fossil records tell us... there may have been life before this!) and the world's land masses began to form. Earth's initial life forms were **bacteria,** which could survive in the highly toxic atmosphere that existed during this time. In fact, all life was bacteria during the Archean Period.

Toward the end of the Archean Period and at the beginning of the Proterozoic Period, about 2.5 billion years ago, oxygen-forming photosynthesis began to occur. The first fossils, in fact, were a type of blue-green **algae** that could photosynthesize. The continents began to form and stabilize, creating the super continent Rodinia about 1.1 billion years ago. (Rodinia is widely accepted as the first super continent, but there were probably others before it.) Although Rodinia is composed of some of the same land fragments as the more popular super continent, Pangaea, they are two different super continents. Pangaea formed some 225 million years ago and would evolve into the seven continents we know today.

By the end of the Proterozoic Period, Earth was well along in its evolutionary process leading to our current period, the Holocene Period, also known as the Age of Man. Thus, about 550 million years ago, the Cambrian Period began. During this period, life "exploded," developing almost all of the **major groups** of plants and animals in a relatively short time. It ended with the massive extinction of most of the existing species about 500 million years ago, making room for the future appearance and evolution of new plant and animal species... Then, about 498 million years later -- 2.2 million years ago -- the **first modern human species** emerged.

3. The mystery of life: from birth to death.

DEATH
Allow me to start with the end!

In one hundred years at the most, we will all be under the earth. There is no way around it! Have a look at this picture and really think about it. Think about your "problems," your worries, your challenges.

Think about when you got upset with your mom or your dad because you wanted to do something and they did not agree, when you made your girlfriend/boyfriend or spouse cry for whatever reason, when you had fear of leaving a perceived security that did not allow you to go after your dreams, when you got angry.

What can you learn? What do you think all people who passed away are telling us? What can we do better? By the way, **this is the niche for a tombstone that could very well be yours or mine.**

Until your time comes, what are you going to do with your life to make it worthwhile? How would you like to be remembered? Would you like your last thought on earth to be one of contentment, realization and peace of mind? If so, start taking massive action towards your dreams right now!

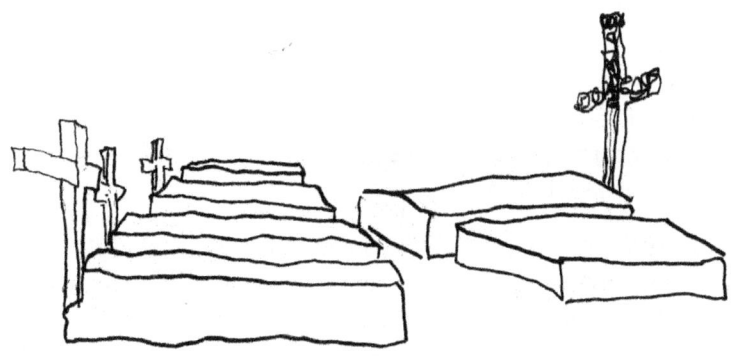

BIRTH
Let us see the amazing development of a baby!

The First Trimester

Very soon after conception, the early placenta begins to develop. By 4 weeks of gestation, the embryo is about 3/8ths of an inch long. Early fetal eyes and limb buds are present by 1 month. Once the fetal heart is completely formed by 6 weeks, it can be seen on an ultrasound.

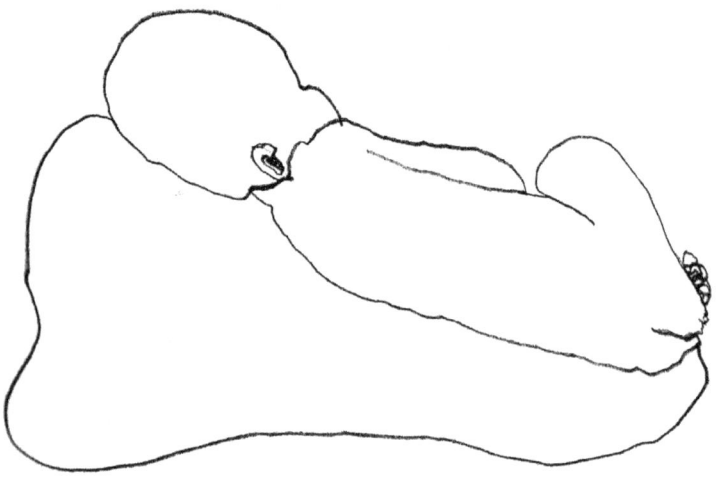

Also, a ridge of tissue, which will become the fetal brain and spinal cord, runs along the embryo's body. At about 5 weeks, urine pregnancy tests can detect HCG, which is secreted by the placenta. This is the basis of a positive pregnancy test. All early fetuses are female. If testes are present, testosterone, the male hormone, is secreted beginning about 8 weeks and those fetuses become male. The rest remain female.

By 10 weeks, all major body organs are present, except for the fetal lungs, which are the last to completely develop. All remaining weeks of gestation are devoted to the growth and maturing of these key body structures. By 12 weeks, the 2-1/2 inch fetus weighs 1-1/2 ounces. The heartbeat can now be heard by listening to the mother's abdomen with a Doppler.

The Second Trimester

By 4 months, the growing fetus weights 7 ounces - just about ½ a pound - and 5 inches from head to rump. The fetus can suck, swallow and make early breathing movements. The arms and legs are completely developed.

At 18 weeks, all body and facial features are recognizable. The eyes begin to blink. The fetus moves quite a lot now, though the mother may not feel it. At 5 months, or 20 weeks, the halfway point in gestation is reached. Soon, the fetus begins to hear the mother's heartbeat and voice. The fetus wakes and sleeps. The fetal sex can be seen with an ultrasound.

The Third Trimester

By 28 weeks, the beginning of the third trimester, the fetus can survive outside of the uterus if the lungs are developed enough. The fetus is usually breech (butt or legs) coming into the pelvis first. At 38 weeks, the lungs are usually mature. The fetus can easily survive outside of the womb. Forty weeks is full term and the average fetus is 20 inches long and weighs 7 pounds. These days, most obstetricians would not let the pregnancy go beyond 42 weeks.

THE AGES OF MAN

Eric Erickson, German psychologist, lived in the 20th century and became very famous for his contribution to our understanding of personality as it is developed and shaped over the course of the lifespan. According to his studies, the human being goes through eight stages.

The First Stage

In the **first 1 and a half years**, the child will develop the virtue of hope – the strong belief that, even when things are not going well, they will work out well in the end. This ability, in later life, gets us through disappointments in love, our careers, and many other domains of life.

Stage Two

Early childhood, from about **eighteen months to three or four years old**. The task is to achieve a degree of autonomy while minimizing shame and doubt. If you get the proper, positive balance of autonomy and shame and doubt, you will develop the virtue of willpower or determination. One of the most admirable and frustrating things about two- and three-year-olds is their determination. "Can do" is their motto. **If we can preserve that "can do" attitude (with appropriate modesty to balance it), we are much better off as adults.**

Stage Three

From **three or four to five or six**, a good balance of initiative without guilt leads to the psychosocial strength of purpose. A sense of purpose is something many people crave in their lives, yet many do not realize that they themselves make their purposes, through imagination and initiative. Perhaps an even better word for this virtue would have been **courage**, the capacity for action despite a clear understanding of your limitations and past failings.

Stage Four

Stage four is the latency stage, or the school-age child from about **six to twelve**. The task is to develop a capacity for industry while avoiding an excessive sense of inferiority. Children must "tame the imagination" and dedicate themselves to education and to learning the social skills their society requires of them, which leads to **competency**.

Stage Five

Adolescence, beginning with puberty and ending around **18 or 20 years old**. The task during adolescence is to achieve **ego identity** and avoid role confusion. It was adolescence that interested Erikson first and most, and the patterns he saw here were the basis for his thinking about all the other stages. If you successfully negotiate this stage, you will have the virtue Erikson called **fidelity**. Fidelity means loyalty, the ability to live by society's standards despite their imperfections, incompleteness and inconsistencies. It also means that you have found a place in that community, a place that will allow you to contribute.

Stage Six

Young adulthood, from about **18 to about 30**. The task is to achieve some **degree of intimacy**, as opposed to remaining in isolation.

If you successfully negotiate this stage, you will carry with you for the rest of your life the virtue or psychosocial strength Erikson calls **love**. It means being able to put aside differences and antagonisms. It includes not only the love we find in a good marriage, but the love between friends and the love of one's neighbor, co-worker, and compatriot.

Stage Seven

Middle adulthood. It is hard to pin a time to it, but it would include the period during which we are actively involved in **raising children**. For most people in our society, this would put it somewhere between the middle twenties and the late fifties. The task here is to cultivate the proper balance of generativity and stagnation.

Generativity is an extension of love into the future. It is a concern for the next generation and all **future generations**. As such, it is considerably less "selfish" than the intimacy of the previous stage: intimacy, the love between lovers or friends, is a love between equals, and it is necessarily reciprocal. Of course, we love each other unselfishly, but the reality is such that, if the love is not returned, we don't consider it a true love. With generativity, that implicit expectation of reciprocity isn't there, at least not as strongly. Few parents expect a "return on their investment" from their children; if they do, we don't think of them as very good parents!

Although the majority of people practice generativity by having and raising children, there are many other ways as well. Erikson considered teaching, writing, invention, the arts and sciences, social activism, and generally contributing to the welfare of future generations to be generativity as well -- anything, in fact, that satisfies that old "need to be needed."

This is the stage of the "**midlife crisis.**" Sometimes men and women take a look at their lives and ask that big, bad question "**what am I doing all this for**?" Look at the question carefully: because their focus is on themselves, they ask what, rather than whom, they are doing it for.

In their panic at getting older and not having experienced or accomplished what they imagined they would when they were younger, they try to recapture their youth.

Men are often the most flamboyant examples: they leave their long-suffering wives, quit their humdrum jobs, buy some "hip" new clothes, and start hanging around singles bars. Of course, they seldom find what they are looking for, because they are looking for the wrong thing! But if you are successful at this stage, you will have a capacity for caring that will serve you through the rest of your life.

Stage Eight

This last one of the stages of life, referred to delicately as late adulthood or maturity, or less delicately as **old age**, begins sometime around retirement, after the kids have gone, say somewhere **around 60**. In Erikson's theory, reaching this stage is a good thing, and not reaching it suggests that earlier problems retarded your development!

First comes a detachment from society, from a sense of usefulness, for most people in our culture. Some retire from jobs they've held for years; others find their duties as parents coming to a close; most find that their input is no longer requested or required.

Then there is a sense of biological uselessness, as the body no longer does everything it used to and the illnesses of old age, such as arthritis, diabetes, heart problems, concerns about breast and ovarian and prostrate cancers. There also come fears about things that one was never afraid of before -- the flu, for example, or just falling down.

Along with the illnesses come concerns of death. Friends die. Relatives die. One's spouse dies. It is, of course, certain that you, too, will have your turn. Faced with all this, it might seem like everyone would feel despair. In response to this despair, some older people become preoccupied with the past. After all, that's where things were better. Some become preoccupied with their failures, the bad decisions they made, and regret that (unlike some in the previous stage) they really don't have the time or energy to reverse them. We find some older people become depressed, spiteful, paranoid, hypochondriacal, or developing the patterns of senility with or without physical bases.

Ego integrity means coming to terms with your life, and thereby coming to terms with the end of life. If you are able to look back and accept the course of events, the choices made, your life as you lived it, as being necessary, then you needn't fear death. Although most of you are not at this point in life, perhaps you can still sympathize by considering your life up to now. We've all made mistakes, some of them pretty nasty ones. Yet, if you hadn't made these mistakes, you wouldn't be who you are. If you had been very fortunate, **or if you had played it safe and made very few mistakes, your life would not have been as rich as it is!**

The maladaptive tendency in stage eight is called presumption. This is what happens when a person "presumes" ego integrity without actually facing the difficulties of old age. The malignant tendency is called disdain, by which Erikson meant a contempt of life; one's own or anyone's. Someone who approaches death without fear has the strength Erikson calls **wisdom**. He called it a gift to children, because "healthy children will not fear life if their elders have integrity enough not to fear death."

Let me share with you a couple of affirmations I find particularly useful to develop wisdom and peace of mind.

1. I **forgive** everyone who can possibly need forgiveness in my life. I **release** all unnecessary situations that are no longer part of the divine plan for my life. I **release** my dreams to the Universe and have absolute faith they will happen in the exact time given.

2. The life in me is perfectly connected with all the life that exists, and it is entirely devoted to **my personal advancement**.

3. The **joy of God** is flowing in me and through me right now and always. **Wisdom** is mine all the time.

4. The mystery of God

What is God? Since the beginning of time man's search for God has never stopped and even today we cannot give very specific answers to that question. We have heard many names: God, Lord, Love, Divine Mind, Jehovah, First Cause, Primal Substance and other names.

Why God? Mankind has always found itself surrounded by uncertainty and conflicts, and it has always searched for strength and wisdom to solve the problems of life.

Let us call God THE LAW. The law of life, the law of mind. All that we may ever desire to have and to be is ours if we apply such principles correctly. Life is not something that just happens to us, we co-create that experience called existence. You must create what you want. Is it more health, wealth, love, happiness, success? Your desires are like seeds you plant in the soil of your mind. Therefore, **plant the thoughts and images of everything you want, cultivate, nurture and guard them well until the harvest comes. Then you will receive all the wonderful rewards of life**.

Dalai Lama differentiates between spirituality and religion. As he explains: "spirituality is there to nourish the human spirit whereas all different religions were designed to make people happier and a better world." He goes on to mention that diversity in religions is necessary, as human beings as well as cultures are very different, but those differences are exactly the ones that should strengthen respect among the people worldwide. He also mentions that the concept of prayer is just a simple daily reminder of principles and values to live by.

Doctor Martin Seligman, father of positive psychology, studied and found out the positive effects of religion and faith on psychological wellbeing. For example, lower probability of drug abuse, crime, divorce and suicide and greater resistance to adversity.

As it has been studied and proved, people who believe in God or experience some kind of spiritual connection, show greater mental strength to face adversity and life crisis. For example, parents with disabled children face depression and despair better and accept circumstances better.

All studies show that those who believe in God are not only happier and more satisfied with life but they also have more resistance and feel less overwhelmed in life crisis: unemployment, divorce, relationship problems, illness and death.

As Mr. Seligman mentions, there is a direct relationship between religion and a healthier and more social character. Furthermore, that link between religious faith and hope for the future explains a great deal of why faith is so valuable to fight despair, resist adversity and become happier.

5. The secret to life. The law of attraction.

This law is creation. Quantum physics tells us that the entire universe emerged from thought and that everyone of us creates his existence and experience with his thoughts.

The law of attraction is an impersonal law of nature. It receives your thoughts and reflects back to you those thoughts as your life experience. It just gives you back what you think about.

Develop prosperity and happiness consciousness. Convince your subconscious mind (affirmations and visualizations) that you are happy, healthy and wealthy and that it feels really good, then your subconscious mind will automatically seek ways of translating your "imaginary" feelings in material form.

Here is the real secret to being and having everything and anything you want:

• First, **ASK** the Universe very clearly what you want. Be very precise, even put a date on it.

• Second, **BELIEVE** you already are in possession of your dream and the law will move people, events and circumstances for you to receive.

• **RECEIVE** means feeling great already for all the good things that will manifest in your life. Be happy, be expectant, do your work, let the universe take care of the details and be a shining star to those around you.

Let me share an example in my personal life. I remember when I first had the general idea of writing a book on the subject happiness. It just came to me! I told the Universe/God I wanted to produce a very practical book that would help the reader become happier. I had the knowledge, I was willing and I was able, so I started to believe I could do it. The actual writing of the book was quite simple, I just let my ego (sense of perfection, preoccupations, should and shouldn't) step out of the way, let the Universal Mind speak through me and the book was manifested right before my eyes!

6. What is reality? A perception issue.

Dear reader, I boldly affirm that "reality does not exist."

You can realize it straight away with a little experiment. Let us say you are sitting on a sofa in your living room, look at the curtains. What do they mean to you? To the husband probably not much. To the wife it may, on the other hand, have a very emotional meaning (wedding present). To the children it may not have any meaning at all but to the young boy or girl studying away from home and seeing again the comfort and warmth of the home, it could mean a world of difference.

You see, what we see in the outside world, we created in our inner world. If you want to be happy, you must realize that we are already happy, we have everything we need within us to feel the joy of being alive on this little planet called earth. Let me show you...

This is the one and only SECRET to HAPPINESS. **Change your mental focus from chasing happiness to being happy**! Do not allow yourself to be happy when you finish university, when you get married, when you have children, when your children grow older, when you get that promotion, when you buy the house, the car, the holidays, when you retire... **be happy now**! Feel gratitude for all the wonderful things in your life, have a dream to improve something you want and try to help your fellow men and women as you walk the path of life. I assure you, that focus shift will mean a world of difference to you and to those around you.

I remember when I had a challenge at work with some co-workers. Instead of feeling resentment, I started praying for them. My mental focus changed, and all of a sudden our relationship improved a great deal.

After applying these principles to my own circumstances and challenges, I finally understood the ancient truth beneath them. I encourage you not to believe me blindly, but to apply it to your own personal world with faith. Keep at it and you will see marvelous results in your life, too.

7. We are beings with unlimited power.

We must realize that every one of us has unlimited power to do anything and everything we dream about. We said earlier that reality does not exist. So, **who told you that you are not able to do what your heart desires?** Was it your family members, your friends, your society, your teachers? Please forget them all and focus on what you can become.

It has been stated by scientists and wise men alike that everything you see in this universe, yourself included, is the expression of an infinite power called **energy**. This power is always flowing into and through you. We can call it energy or Spirit. I show you how to tap into this power. Every morning and night, I do my relaxation and meditation ritual. It takes about ten minutes and it is one the best exercises you can do. Take the following steps and I assure you, that you will begin to feel unconquerable and full of energy:

1. **Relax**. Breathe in and out several times and think, "I am relaxed."

2. **The healing light**. Count from five to one. The moment you reach one, see a bright, marvelous and spiritual light in front of you. This is the Universal Mind itself. This is the place of absolute peace of mind, your sacred temple, where you can rest and ask for anything. It will grant you anything you need. **Believe it!** I have had psoriasis for twenty years. It is a skin disorder. I have used all types of creams, and it wasn't until I began to use healing meditation that the skin problems started to disappear. I imagine two healing hands applying a healing cream to the bad spots. Both are made of this wonderful, all-powerful, healing light.

3. **Forgiveness and gratitude**. I forgive myself first and anyone who might need my forgiveness, and I feel free. I thank God for the uncountable blessings in my life.

4. **Dream visualization**. I visualize my dreams being accomplished.

5. **Good wishes to humanity**. I send good wishes to all my

loved ones, friends, co-workers and humanity.

6. **Daily activities**. I go on with my daily activities full of enthusiasm.

8. **What is fear, and what to do about it?**

I know a bit about fear. I have had fear of doing things, of saying things and of trying things all my life. I presume I am not much different than the rest of my fellow men and women. However, what I have learned is that the important thing is not whether you feel fear, doubt, anxiety, but what you do with it. Please, do not let fear stand in the way of your dreams. If you do that, you will regret it for the rest of your days. Be bold, be courageous, be outrageous. Do not tiptoe around fear. Step on it, stumble across fear, laugh at it, **feel the fear and do it anyway!** I assure you, that uneasy feeling called fear will disappear the moment you decide nothing will stand in the way of dreams. By the way, fear is just a mental perception, an illusion. **Are you going to put your destiny and the one of your family in the hands of a mental illusion?**

You know? The cemeteries are full of people who were going to chase their dreams some day but never even started. Why? Because they had fear. Fear of changing, fear of losing a certain amount of "security" and fear of living outside their "comfort zone." What do kids do to learn skating, for example? They get up every time they fall. What about a bumblebee? It is physically impossible for this insect to fly, as its body is too heavy and its wings to small. They can fly because they think they can fly. **What miracles are you able to perform?**

Let me give you a **tool bag** to overcome fear. **Mentally,** know what you want and take the first step. The whole road will unfold as you start taking steps. Know where you are and where you are going. Use the power of concentrating your actions, like a laser. **Emotionally**, listen to your heart when you define the goal, forget the past, focus on your wonderful future and follow your dreams. **Take action**: do not allow anything to stand in the way of your aspirations. Live, enjoy and make the most out of the present moment. DO IT NOW! You are the master of your destiny.

We were given the gift of life. Live, love, enjoy every second of your existence and leave the world better than you found it. You will become a happy human being, you will make those around happier **and the world will smile because you lived!**

9. What would you do if you could not fail and had all the money and resources in the world?

The next time you find yourself relaxing on the couch and watching your favorite film, ask yourself this question: "What would you do if you won $1,000,000 in the lottery? Would you work? If you knew anything you touched or did held the possibility of success, what would you do? If there were no time restrictions, no obstacles, no self-doubt, what would you do? Some of you might say that is not possible or is very unlikely. The whole point is to get your imagination expanding. The first thing to do is to **imagine** your ideal life without restrictions. The second step is to ask yourself: "**Am I willing? Am I able?**" If the answer is yes to both questions, the last step is to make a **plan** for the next five years and take daily action towards its realization. Review progress, do not despair if things do not turn out as planned and have faith in yourself and God. Believe in the laws of the universe we will discuss in the last chapter. They work in the same way as the physical laws if you understand how to apply them. If you do not reach your goals in the planned deadline, change the time, but do not change the goal. The only failure in life is giving up.

As **Anthony Robbins**, bestseller author of "**Awaken the Giant Within**" mentioned, there are several concepts you should consider. The best technique to achieving extraordinary results is to perform at your most productive emotional state. **First**, if you change your body, you change your emotional state. For example, every time you feel a bit depressed, take a walk at fast pace, shoulders up, head high and your eyes looking straight. It is impossible to feel depressed that way. **Second**, change your mental focus from negativity to positive results. You feel empowered and full of hope immediately. **Last**, fill your life with activities that make you a happier and more fulfilled person.

"**Change your focus and you change your life!**"
Oscar Escallada

10. What are you going to do and how are you going to live the remaining days and hours you have been given on this earth?

Dear reader, the most valuable resource we have is **TIME**. You are going to live only once. What are you going to do? Let me explain. I am 40 years old. This means I have lived 14,600 days, 350,640 hours, I have slept approximately 116,800 hours and been awake **233,760 hours**. I hope to reach age 100, but in case I only live 80 years, I have 233,760 hours awake left and then I will be gone. **I am determined to make the most out of it, and you? Please see how many hours you have left and make your life count, for you, your loved ones, your community and the world.**

Age Chart (Years-Days-Hours)				
Years	Days	Hours	1/3 Sleeping	Hours awake
1	365	8,766	2,922	5,844
10	3,650	87,660	29,220	58,440
15	5,475	131,400	43,800	87,600
20	7,300	175,320	58,440	116,880
25	9,125	219,000	73,000	146,000
30	10,950	262,980	87,660	175,320
35	12,775	306,600	102,200	204,400
40	14,600	350,640	116,880	233,760
45	16,425	394,200	131,400	262,800
50	18,250	438,300	146,100	292,200
55	20,075	481,800	160,600	321,200
60	21,900	525,960	175,320	350,640
65	23,725	568,400	189,466	378,933
70	25,550	613,620	204,540	409,080

You Were Born Happy!

Age Chart (Years-Days-Hours)				
Years	Days	Hours	1/3 Sleeping	Hours awake
75	27,375	657,000	219,000	438,000
80	29,200	701,280	233,760	467,520
85	31,025	744,600	248,200	496,400
90	32,855	788,940	262,980	525,960
100	36,500	876,660	292,220	584,440

WHAT DO YOU REALLY WANT?

DREAM BIG, FEEL UNCONQUERABLE AND TAKE MASSIVE ACTION

YOUR DAYS ARE NUMBERED ANYWAY!!!

DO YOU WANT TO HAVE IT ALL?

START RIGHT NOW – YOU ARE RUNNING OUT OF TIME

THINK OF 30 GOALS YOU WOULD LIKE TO ACCOMPLISH IN YOUR LIFE

CHOOSE THE 3 MOST IMPORTANT ONES

WRITE 5 SPECIFIC ACTIONS YOU WILL DO EVERY DAY TO ACHIEVE THOSE 3 GOALS AND DO THEM WITH DISCIPLINE

I ASSURE YOU YOUR DREAMS WILL MANIFEST

1. ACTION 1 _____

2. ACTION 2 _____

3. ACTION 3 _____

4. ACTION 4 _____

5. ACTION 5 _____

1. THOUGHTS

How can you learn to think clearly in order to have peace of mind, focus on your dreams, solve problems and enjoy life?

GOD JUPITER
Choose your thoughts and you choose your life

**King of the gods and ruler of Mount Olympus;
God of the sky and thunder**

1. Who are you?

From low self-esteem to extraordinary self-image and confidence

2. What do you want?

From confusion and indecisiveness to absolute clarity and the power of decision

3. How to make your chosen path the best option?

From indifference and lack of faith to commitment and the unstoppable strength of belief

4. How can you recover strength when you fall?

From boredom and inefficiency to enthusiasm and efficiency

5. How to apply the laws of the universe?

From under achievement and ignorance to producing results and acquiring wisdom in life

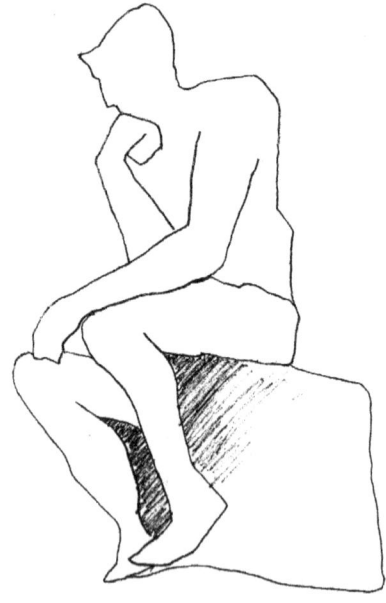

WHO ARE YOU?

1.1 FROM LOW SELF-ESTEEM TO YOUR EXTRAORDINARY WINNER'S IMAGE

From night-shift receptionist in Madrid in 2004 to general hotel manager in Cuba in 2011

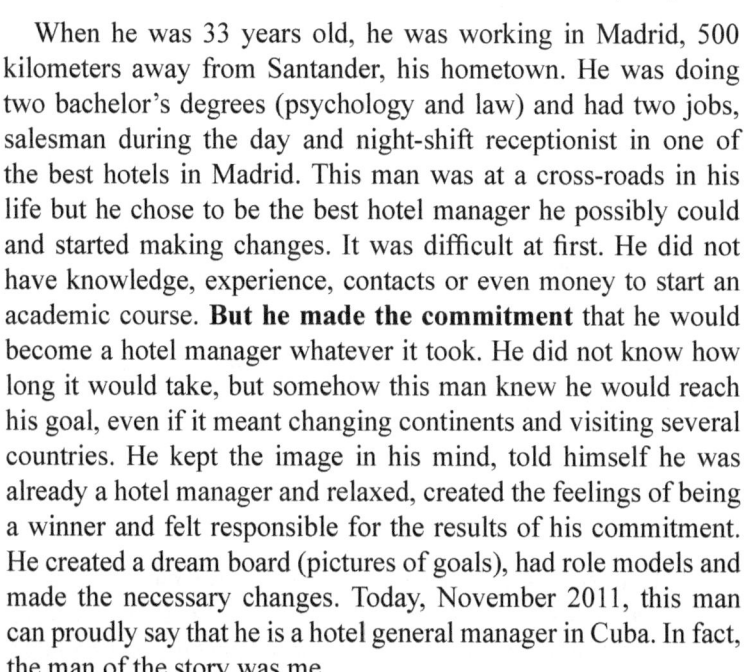

Science and psychology have isolated the one primary cause for success or failure in life. It is the hidden self-image that you have of yourself. Your success in any undertaking will never be greater than the image you have of yourself. Let me tell you the story of someone who dramatically changed his life.

When he was 33 years old, he was working in Madrid, 500 kilometers away from Santander, his hometown. He was doing two bachelor's degrees (psychology and law) and had two jobs, salesman during the day and night-shift receptionist in one of the best hotels in Madrid. This man was at a cross-roads in his life but he chose to be the best hotel manager he possibly could and started making changes. It was difficult at first. He did not have knowledge, experience, contacts or even money to start an academic course. **But he made the commitment** that he would become a hotel manager whatever it took. He did not know how long it would take, but somehow this man knew he would reach his goal, even if it meant changing continents and visiting several countries. He kept the image in his mind, told himself he was already a hotel manager and relaxed, created the feelings of being a winner and felt responsible for the results of his commitment. He created a dream board (pictures of goals), had role models and made the necessary changes. Today, November 2011, this man can proudly say that he is a hotel general manager in Cuba. In fact, the man of the story was me.

"**Reality does not exist! What do you want in life? Who do you want to be? Well...DO IT AND BE IT. There is no tomorrow.**"
Oscar Escallada

1.2 FROM LOW TO HIGH CONFIDENCE

THE 10-STEP CHALLENGE

THOUGHTS

1. Take an inventory. What do you want to improve? Make one change at a time.

2. Pay more attention to other people than to yourself. Be caring.

3. Stay, as some would say, "in the moment." Focus on the other person 100% during a conversation.

FEELINGS

4. Celebrate your journey, not your destination. Learn to always feel good about where you are now.

5. Know that you will reach your goals with work and persistence.

6. Feel the joy of sharing a part of your life with someone you know or you have just met.

ACTIONS

7. Do what you love and you will feel good immediately.

8. Help others do what they cannot do for themselves and lead others by example, taking the first step in the right direction. Promote communication, generosity and interest in other people's lives.

9. Improve yourself. Learn to change from being competitive to being creative. Competition with others only leads to permanent frustration. Be honest with yourself and the world.

10. Be proactive and positive. Go towards people loving yourself and take actions that are positive for yourself and others. Be yourself.

Remember, if you want to change anything in your life, you will keep getting the same results until the very moment you create and hold in your mind the person you want to become.

"I asked my counselor once about my vocation. I asked: How can I know if God is calling me and what for? He answered: you will know by your level of happiness. That will be the evidence of your vocation."
Mother Teresa

WHAT DO YOU WANT?

1.3 FROM CONFUSION TO ABSOLUTE CLARITY

The birth and creation of the Body Shop

In 1976 Anita Roddick had the idea of opening a shop to sell cosmetics with natural components. She opened her first shop in Brighton, England, and when she did, the other shop owners in the neighborhood used to bet on how long she would survive. She had many difficulties (she could not find deliverers, had no enough capital or marketing experience) but she managed to succeed internationally.

Anita changed the awareness of her potential, forgot the past results and focused only on success. She understood the power behind dissatisfaction, believed in feeling happy no matter the circumstances and chose her heart's desire as the guiding rule towards her peace of mind. Besides, she focused all her efforts on one specific and powerful must (as opposed to mere wishes) and visualized her goal over and over again.

Nowadays, The Body Shop has more than 1,500 shops all over the world, its value is over 500 million US dollars and it has influenced the products and businesses of its main competitors.

She has also awaken social consciousness over environment care and support to local communities in underdeveloped countries. Furthermore, all employees worldwide receive half a day of work a month to participate in social activities to help the community.

As Anita said: "What saved us over and over was the attitude of realizing what wasn't working, improving it and making it happen. Being flexible and open to creative solutions has produced marvelous results all along the history of the company."

"Decide what you want. Decide what you are prepared to give up to get it. Set your mind on it. Get on with the work."
H.L. Hunt

1.4 FROM INDECISIVENESS TO THE POWER OF DECISION

THE 10-STEP CHALLENGE

One of the saddest human situations I encounter is the emotional wars some people suffer due to ambivalence. Leave-don't leave, say it-don't say it, do it-don't it, go-don't go. The main problem is clarity, the courage to make it and the commitment to follow through.

THOUGHTS

1. **Realize the power of your mind**. The conscious part has an incredible analysis potential. However, any image/idea you fix through repetition or impact on your subconscious mind, will create anything you desire.

2. Be true to yourself, do not let others (society, teachers, parents, friends, lovers, etc...) tell you what you can or cannot do.

3. We experience reality through our five senses (see, hear, smell, taste and touch), but we also have six mental faculties to fulfill our dreams (intuition, imagination, perception, reason, memory and will).

FEELINGS

4. Happiness is not really a goal but the result of being aware that prosperity is the manifestation of exciting and service-oriented goals.

5. Feeling is the language of the subconscious mind. Whatever desire you may have is the force of an unexpressed possibility within you, attempting to become physical reality.

6. Through reason you will adapt to the changes and a new awareness will be formed. Only then will you see the next step on your way.

ACTIONS

7. Make a written description of the three most important goals and make it your top priority to achieve them.

8. Do what your feelings tell you to do. Old habits will fade away as new habits consolidate with disciple and persistence.

9. Decision Check: do you really want it and don't harm anyone?

10. Make your motto: "**I Just do it until I reach the goal.**"

"Life is either a daring adventure or nothing."
Helen Keller

MAKING THE CHOSEN PATH THE BEST OPTION!

1.5. FROM INDIFFERENCE TO COMMITMENT

A miracle was needed and he created it!

The surgeon who operated with his feet!

One of the biggest earthquakes in history (8.1 Richter scale) took place in Mexico City in September, 1985, taking more than 4,200 lives. Francisco Bucio was a plastic surgeon who was trapped in the wreckage and lost his right hand, but

his dream of being a great surgeon did not die. He looked for the best specialists in the field and went through several intense operations. He had two of his toes transplanted onto his right hand. It took firm determination, countless hours of rehabilitation and iron commitment until he could operate at professional level. Today he is a top surgeon and helps the poor as a volunteer.

Intellectually, he was aware that there is an infinite supply of spirit. We are all spirit, endowed with the unique ability to originate thought and reach any goal. He was also aware that true wealth is the unlimited creative power we all have and that working for satisfaction is one of life's true joys. **Emotionally**, such passion gave him a sense of relief and purpose in life and he realized that he was in charge of creating his emotions, not allowing anything or anyone cause his feelings. Besides, he took **massive action** towards his dream. He made a binding commitment to himself, planned the actions and reviewed the progress, focused on his goal and was grateful for every second of his life.

Francisco said: "In life we face different challenges. However, if we let our deepest passion guide us as inspiration, we will overcome any obstacle and make our dreams come true."

"Doing at once what needs to be done will ensure the possibility of success."
Leland Val Van De Wall

1.6. FROM LACK OF FAITH TO THE UNSTOPPABLE STRENGTH OF BELIEF

THOUGHTS

1. Remove mental blocks by creating the space for the beautiful images you are trying to create. The vacuum law of prosperity (nature abhors a vacuum) tells us that we must let go of the old, before we can even make room for the new.

2. **What is worthy of you** to dedicate your life to and enjoy every minute of it? Your mind is a center of divine operation. You receive countless ideas from the universal mind. You just have to believe, take action and let go.

3. Follow your dream. This is the creative process. You retain your vision, focus on your purpose and be grateful. The "how" is God's job.

FEELINGS

4. Both science and religion agree that there is a source energy from where everything comes. That source works through you. So, expect the good that you desire, understand that desire is divine and doubt is only fear in disguise.

5. Make use of the deductive reasoning, the subconscious mind. It has no ability to reject ideas, images or suggestions. It causes you to vibrate in a certain way and attract what you put in your subconscious mind. So, accept only the ideas that will improve the quality of your life.

6. Destroy doubt with faith. Have and develop a strong sense of faith in yourself and the ability to achieve what you imagine.

ACTIONS

7. Make a list of the areas in your physical world in which you will create a vacuum. Write the date as a deadline to create the space. For example, get rid of all the old clothes in your closet for new ones to come.

8. Make a goal card (a little card with a picture or affirmation on it) of your heart's desire and take steps towards it.

9. Be positive to others: smile, inspire, help and be more humane.

10. Be creative, enjoy the present, fight for your beliefs, be responsible and make others believe in themselves and their dreams.

> "What a wonderful life I had! I wished I had realized before."
> Colette, French novelist of XX century

RECOVERING STRENGTH WHEN YOU FALL

1.7 FROM BOREDOM TO ENTHUSIASM

From feeling bored to "the enthusiastic Man"

Dear reader, I have had my share of frustration, failures and boredom, but I learned how to find the motivation that would inspire me for the rest of my days. When I was thirteen years old I promised myself I would only focus on being enthusiastic about life. In the last twenty years, I have been asked so many times where I get the energy from. It is the desire to be more, to enjoy life more and to love more.

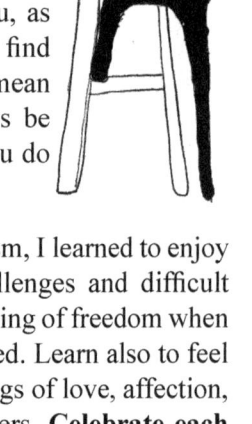

Three concepts helped me a lot. One, choose what things, people and events mean to you, as reality is a subjective phenomenon. Two, find your gift and share it with the world, it will mean heaven on earth for you. And third, always be yourself, think for yourself, be authentic, you do not have to impress anybody.

On my search for the meaning of enthusiasm, I learned to enjoy not only the good things but also the challenges and difficult situations, as you experience a wonderful feeling of freedom when the problem is solved and the lesson is learned. Learn also to feel satisfaction for life, fill your heart with feelings of love, affection, optimism, curiosity and compassion for others. **Celebrate each day as "the best day of your life," and it will be so.**

I invite you to do the following: **do visualizations three times a day** for five minutes, seeing and feeling all the marvelous things in your life, present and future. Do what you love doing and the money will follow; this means, find the time to do that passion of yours, even a few minutes a day, take your time to become better and better, find ways to reach the public and the money will come. Increase your strengths and diminish your weaknesses. Above all, always keep the flame burning of creating a better world for you, your loved ones and the whole world.

"Seest thou a man diligent in his business? He shall stand before kings."
Proverbs 22:29

1.8 FROM INEFFICIENCY TO EFFICIENCY

THOUGHTS

1. Do you really want to produce extraordinary results in your life? Do not allow present results or circumstances to control the image of your dream. Just start somewhere. The steps will unfold one at a time.

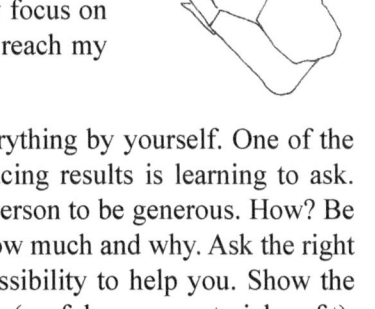

2. Have good mental tools for the journey: I can is my motto, I only focus on solutions not on problems, I will reach my goal whatever it takes!

3. You do not have to do everything by yourself. One of the most important abilities in producing results is learning to ask. In so doing, you allow the other person to be generous. How? Be honest. Be specific about what, how much and why. Ask the right person: someone who has the possibility to help you. Show the person the benefit he/she will gain (usefulness or material profit). Finally, be thankful and return the favor as soon as you can.

FEELINGS

4. Feel the risk and the fear of doing that thing you really desire and do it anyway. From today onwards you are a dynamic risk-taker full of energy, only focusing on your dream, your strengths and your assets.

5. **From where you are to where you want to go**, you will have to go through the terror barrier. That is the place outside your comfort zone. The more you are there, the less effect it will have on you.

6. Be proud of belonging to those who accomplish things. The world is full of those who almost made it by an inch.

ACTIONS

7. List six actions you will do immediately that will make a difference in your life and will solve the problem or improve the situation.

8. Use Pareto's principle: 20% of your work create 80% of the results, focus on that 20% to increase productivity.

9. Have your own code of excellence and be a model, first to improve yourself and feel proud and then for your loved ones and the world.

10. Have a plan to manage what you do with your valuable time.

"If you do not like something, change it. If you cannot change it, change your attitude. Do not complain."
Maya Angelou

APPLYING THE LAWS OF THE UNIVERSE!

1.9 FROM UNDER ACHIEVEMENT TO RESULTS

The man on a mission from Africa to England!

In 1958 Legson Kayra from the remote village of Niasaland in Africa had a dream, he wanted to be like his hero Abraham Lincoln, leave poverty behind and serve humanity. He was 16 years old, no money, no education and no contacts. He forgot everything except his dream, going to university in the United States of America.

He started a 3,000-mile and two-year journey to Cairo, going through a thousand calamities. When people in different parts of the world learnt from his dream and determination, the legend had already started and all the pieces of the puzzle started to fit in. He received an invitation to a university in America, the plane ticket was paid by funds raised by students and the paperwork was taken care of by missionaries who taught him in his childhood. At the end, he became a university professor and writer in the field of politics.

Legson knew what success meant to him and that **it was just a matter of time and persistence**, he kept being flexible until the end and realized that you can always do better than the present results you are getting. Meeting his basic needs gave him security, but the hunger for adventure told him to keep moving forward. His emotional strength was based on the magic of the right attitude, which creates excitement and dissolves frustration and guilt for past failures instantly. He kept taking action, reviewing what was done, rethinking next steps and redefining his goal. He rewarded himself mentally by seeing himself over and over again being accountable to his loved ones saying, "I made it," and he realized the power of being surrounded by people who support you in the different steps of the way.

"A mind focused on doubt and fear cannot focus on the journey to victory."
Mike Jones.

1.10 FROM IGNORANCE TO WISDOM

The universal laws in my work

In the same way that there are physical laws (gravity, pressure, electricity, etc…) we should be aware of the Laws of Life. Nature is always successful. Taking nature as our model, we can live in harmony with these laws to lead a better life. How did I create spectacular results at work with The Laws? (Created great work atmosphere, improved

client satisfaction in hotels in different parts of the world and received the Green Globe certification for good environmental practices in Mexico).

THOUGHTS

1. **The Law of Perpetual Transmutation.**

I held the image of success with different teams and that came to pass.

2. **The Law of Relativity.**

I was never fearful of a negative outcome. Everything is relative.

3. **The Law of Thinking**

Lead by example with a positive attitude and the world follows.

FEELINGS

4. **The Law of Vibration (Attraction).**

Your thoughts create your feelings, actions and your end results.

5. **The Law of Rhythm.**

There are ups and downs. Always think of the good times coming.

6. The Law of Compensation.

Whatever you sow, you reap. Simple and very true.

ACTIONS
7. The Law of Polarity.

Good and Bad. I prefer to only focus on the good all the time.

8. The Law of Gender.

From an idea to its realization there is a period of work and patience.

9. The Law of Cause and Effect.

Whatever you send into the Universe comes back to you tenfold.

10. The Law of Success.

If you think you can, you can and will succeed in any field.

"The wisdom acquired with the passage of time is a useless gift unless you share it."
Esther Williams

2. FEELINGS

What emotions do you want to feel? How can you cope with negative emotions and constantly experience positive feelings?

GODDESS JUNO

**Ask yourself, what would love do
and the answer will always be right**

**Queen of the gods and the goddess
of marriage, family and love**

1. **Do you want to have good memories of the past?**

From regret and blindness to pride and gratitude

2. **Do you want to enjoy the present moment?**

From sadness and unhappiness to joy and happiness

3. **How can you have love in all areas of your life?**

From lack of affection and selfishness to love and contribution

4. **How do you avoid pain and gain pleasure?**

From hesitation and passivity to determination and passion

5. **What does your future look like?**

From worry and pessimism to hope and optimism

GOOD MEMORIES OF THE PAST

2.1 FROM REGRET TO PRIDE

Back to the future, year 2051

I would like to live 100 years. It is now 2011 and I am 40 years old, so **I imagine I am 90 years of age**, sitting on a rocking chair, looking at a beautiful sunset from the entrance of my home and reflecting on my life. You know, I am glad that I allowed my heart to lead me and, above all, I feel proud of myself that I have no regrets.

Let us apply the same reasoning to your past now. Why should you regret anything? The best thing is to accept failures as part of the learning process and move on. Love yourself unconditionally by accepting the imperfect nature of your being. What happened that makes you feel so bad? **Leave the past in the past**, learn from the experience and try to teach others.

What do you do with those feelings of anger, sadness and guilt? **Anger** means that an important rule was violated by someone and the best antidote is forgiveness. Your ability to forgive makes you a better person, empties your heart of negative emotions and makes you free and happy in an instant. **Sadness** normally tells us that we miss someone. Realize your feelings are noble, be the best you can be and make them proud. If **guilt** appears, make the commitment not to repeat any behavior that may cause such feeling.

I have a way of feeling proud of myself. I always try to listen to myself. **Happiness is a teacher**. It teaches me what I like and what I want. You just have to listen and have the courage to follow through. I have passion for the things I do, and I love that feeling! I take care of my loved ones and am respectful with the rest of the world around me.

"The price of greatness is responsibility."
Winston Churchill

2.2 FROM BLINDNESS TO GRATITUDE

THOUGHTS

1. **Open your eyes to the abundance of the Universe**. The key to happiness is the attitude of gratitude for all we have and are, and for everything we do not have and think is impossible to achieve. It is the most efficient way to produce miracles and make our dreams come true.

2. Get your priorities right, do not take yourself too seriously and be aware of all you have achieved.

3. Remember that what you focus on expands. If you want more good things in your life, be thankful for everything.

FEELINGS

4. Enjoy all moments of the day, forget past grievances and hope for the best in the near and far future.

5. Remember we are 90% water and we react in the same way. According to studies, if you send love and gratitude to water drops, beautiful and symmetric structures form, but if you send negative vibrations, formless figures are created.

6. **Love yourself**, it is the most important thing you can do in life, and be true to yourself. In the last minutes of your life, you will be blessed if you can say to yourself your life was the expression of your inner desires, regardless of the circumstances.

ACTIONS

7. **Express gratitude** for life every chance you have, and be thankful to your fellowmen and women on every opportunity.

8. Keep a diary with writings and pictures of all the things, situations and people you are grateful for, past, present and future.

9. Treat every person you meet as the most important person on earth, with respect and dignity, you are spreading joy around you.

10. Do your morning gratitude ritual. The emotional state you get up with sets the tone for the rest of the day. I say, "Thank you, Lord, for my health, for my family and my friends, for my wonderful profession, for my girlfriend and for my passion for life."

"The best thing to do with the best things in life is to give them up."
Dorothy Day

ENJOYING THE PRESENT NOW

2.3 FROM SADNESS TO JOY– Wake up, your life is waiting!

I read a very interesting story I would like to share with you. A wise man was talking to the richest businessman in town who was wearing very expensive clothes, shoes and jewelry. The businessman asked, "What do I have to give up to experience real happiness and inner peace?" The wise man said, "I have good and bad news. The good news is that you do not have to give up any of the things you have. Poverty is not the way to happiness; the bad news, though, is that you have to do something much more difficult: **change your thoughts and you change your heart**, and in return, you change your behavior, your results and how people treat you."

Erase sadness from your consciousness, there are a thousand things to be interested in and hope for! Use the power of your incredible mind and start living the joy of life. **First**, question your thoughts. We have about 60,000 thoughts a day, one per second and 80% are negative. When you analyze your negative thoughts and realize you do not have to believe them, you wipe out unhappiness straight away. **Second**, use the **Sedona method**: Eliminate the feelings created by a negative thought NOW. **Third**, focus only on positive thoughts and discard negative ones.

Invite cheerfulness into your life, make excitement your best friend and realize dissatisfaction can make you transform your life.

Do this. Make a life's plan with 100 things you would like to do or achieve before you die. Then make a long list of the little things that make you a bit happier. Keep a record of your negative beliefs, question them, look for evidence to prove to yourself that they are not true. Use the Sedona method when necessary.

"Most folks are about as happy as they make up their minds to be."
Abraham Lincoln

2.4 FROM UNHAPPINESS TO HAPPINESS

I remember one night when I was a kid, my grandmother told me about the great battle that takes place in the innermost part of every human being. "Dear son, it is a fight between two wolves that live inside us. One is unhappiness—fear, worry, guilt, hatred, resentment, inferiority and envy. The other is happiness—compassion, love, hope, optimism, joy, gratitude, kindness and generosity." After a while, I asked, "And who wins this battle?" My grandma looked at me with compassionate eyes and said, "**The one you feed, dear son.**" Thank you granny, I will never forget your wise words!

THOUGHTS

1. I am a millionaire because I can enjoy everything in the world and I accept myself with strengths and weaknesses, I am my best friend.

2. Fill up your mind with so many and so beautiful thoughts that any negative thought daring to enter your mind, will flee away.

3. With negative thoughts? Just let them come and go, they have no power over you whatsoever. You are in charge of your life!

FEELINGS

4. Love yourself and think about your happiness first, a happy person is a gift to the rest of the world, his family, friends and society.

5. Do everything with joy and joy will be everywhere for you.

6. Make serenity and peace of mind your allies. From now on, have the security that **life is a marvelous one-way journey you came to enjoy.**

ACTIONS

7. Do your daily meditation on happiness. Example: "Thank you God for everything in my life, past, present and my future."

8. Act today as the happiest person you have ever known. Do it one day at a time and you will become that person.

9. Practice flow, getting mentally lost in an activity you enjoy a lot.

10. Do you want to live in a happier world and be happier yourself? Pass the gift on, leave every person you come in contact with happier than you found him/her. I am sure you know how to do it.

> "To love what you do and feel that it matters, how could anything be more fun?"
> Katherine Graham

2.5 FROM LACK OF AFFECTION TO LOVE

According to studies carried out by Edward Diener, father of investigation on happiness and Martin Seligman, founder of positive psychology, a common characteristic of happier people is that they all had friends and an intimate relationship with another person. In fact, our brain has been programmed to relate to others, that is why emotions are contagious.

This is the story of Peter Hernandez, a friend of mine. As a teenager he used to be alone, did not have many friends, was not very good-looking and did not have much success either in sports or academics, until one day the most popular guy at school, John Sanchez, decided to help Peter. They became friends, talked a lot and agreed on the following plan:

John told Peter that his grandmother had told him to keep three secrets in mind in order to **be popular and have a lot of friends**. **First**, accept yourself the way you are, there is no one like you and everyone has a gift to offer to the world. **Second**, find balance in life: health, money, love, relations, profession, spirituality. **Third**, focus on the positive aspects of other people, not on the negative.

John also advised him to watch his feelings. Be caring and compassionate with others, everyone needs a bit of help. If you ever feel hurt, change your perception of the situation or talk to the person involved and the feeling will disappear in a matter of seconds. Above all, show respect for every human being and it will dissipate any negative feelings like envy, rage, hostility and disappointment among others. Besides, John added, "Surround yourself with support, be a good listener, raise your capacity to love and consider the world your family, as it truly is." After many years,

Peter asked John why he had wanted to help him and John answered, "**Because you helped me become a better person.**" I was having dinner with them that day. It was just wonderful!

"**The gift of happiness belongs to those who give it.**"
Anonymous

2.6 FROM SELFISHNESS TO CONTRIBUTION

THOUGHTS

1. Imagine what a **better world** it would be if all of us cultivated a sense of helping those around us!

2. It is said that the secret of living is giving. Bear it in mind and your life will be transformed. One of the richest emotions is when you enhance life's experience for someone you care about or someone you don't even know yet.

3. **How do you want to be remembered**? As a giant among men? Start right now! Live each day as if it were one of the most important days of your life. Make your life memorable, for you, your loved ones, your friends and all the people around you!

FEELINGS

4. You do not want to create feelings of gloominess and inferiority in your children. They need a strong self-image, they need satisfaction, shared joy, laughter, play, the security of alternatives and unconditional acceptance.

5. Who has not felt stupid or bored at school? Teachers should build the children's confidence on every occasion.

6. Society's constant materialistic messages make us feel we are not good enough. Accept yourself just the way you are, you do not need to look younger, buy the latest product or know everything.

ACTIONS

7. Make kindness a way of living. You can give everything: a helping hand, a comforting word, your company and your time.

8. Look for ways to help and you will find them: environment, prisons, homelessness, hospitals, community programs, counseling.

9. Smile, laugh and make people laugh at any opportunity you may have, for it is free and it makes a world of difference to people. Dress as a clown and make children laugh and watch funny movies.

10. The best thing you can do for society is **be happy**, be an example for others to follow, expressing that life is a gift from God and that our gift back to God is to make the most out of this incredible experience for ourselves and others.

"If we have no peace, it is because we have forgotten that we belong to each other."
Mother Teresa

2.7 FROM HESITATION TO DETERMINATION

How this book was written

The actual story of this book will illustrate very well how I went from hesitation to determination. My experience with self-help books started when I was 17 years old and spent one year in the United States with an American family. I completed the last year of High School in the state of Indiana. It was the first time I left my home country and my family, and it was a very hard year for me. I was not able to communicate in English during the first four months of my stay. So, I became involved in this kind of books and it helped a lot to focus my mind.

Later in life, I studied psychology but no single subject dealt with the topic of happiness, so I used to go to the public library and devour all the books I could find on leading a more fulfilling life. By age 37, the idea of writing my own book entered my mind. At first I hesitated. Thoughts like: Who do you think you are to write a book?, WHAT do you know about happiness?, HOW on earth do I get started?, ran through my mind all the time However, like all important decisions in life, there comes a time, a threshold, **a breakthrough**, when you say: "I had it, I will take the control." I made the decision and gained confidence. I kept being flexible, reading, writing, rewriting and never allowed anything to spoil my dream.

I went through valleys of frustration and inadequacy, at times disappointment but never lost heart. God planted this little seed in me and I was determined to finish the project, whatever it took. Besides, the natural curiosity of creating a valuable product never left me and helped me in the dark moments of doubt.

In the process, I learnt to lead by example and walk my talk, to do whatever I did in life with joy, to develop strength and to be persistent. As they say, no other ability is more closely related to success than persistence, it is only a matter of time.

"Belief and your belief will create the fact."
William James

2.8 FROM PASSIVITY TO PASSION

Passion and excitement can add power to anything we want. But you need to know what you are passionate about first.

THOUGHTS

1. What is your hobby, what do you like, what do you admire in other people that they do, what did you use to love when you were a kid, what do you dislike so much that you want to change?

2. **Visualize your target with a lot of emotion** and imagination, start somewhere (you don't need to know all the way, just the next steps ahead), take specific actions and review your progress.

3. Whether you think you are fine with that boring job that does not even provide you with the necessary economic resources you need to lead a happy life with your loved ones or whether you think it is better to give it a try and find an interesting activity, where you feel useful, create a great service and has the potential of high income, **you are right**, your mental life is yours, you decide.

FEELINGS

4. Listen to your emotions, especially the negative ones. What are they trying to tell you? They are leading you to your destination.

5. When you **find your passion**, thousand negative emotions banish once and for all; depression, sadness, envy, resentment. There is only place in your heart for providing the best possible service to the world.

6. You must get out of your passive comfort zone. It will be a bit uncomfortable at first but that is the way to grow as a person.

ACTIONS

7. How do you do it? Just like everything else, you make a decision. Deciding is giving up other options and concentrating effort.

8. Get involved with an idea-project bigger than yourself, you will need it to gather up strength when the storm comes.

9. Get the motivation of the dream or dissatisfaction, raise your curiosity, explore new possibilities and keep moving forward.

10. Research, try, make mistakes until you find the purpose that will make your eyes shine with enthusiasm and your life heaven on earth.

"Always be a first-rate version of yourself, instead of a second-rate version of somebody else."
Judy Garland

LOOKING AT A BRIGHT FUTURE

2.9 FROM WORRY TO HOPE

The story of Oprah Winfrey

Oprah Winfrey discovered her talent at a very early age, talking and listening with empathy, but had a very hard childhood. She was born in rural Mississippi and was raised by her grandmother. During that time she suffered physical and emotional abuse. As a teenager, she used drugs and had an abortion, and it was her strict father that made her come to terms with her life.

She then realized that all her troubles were due to lack of confidence and worry of what people could think of her. From a television reporter, she went on to talk show presenter and actress. She realized worry did not serve her at all, gained perspective and focused on solutions. She has been considered by Time magazine to be one of the top hundred most influential people in the twentieth century and Forbes magazine called her the first black millionaire woman.

She has many times mentioned that you have the power to change your life, you are the only one who is responsible for everything in your life, your health, your wealth and your happiness and that there is always a possibility for success and it always starts in you.

She is an example of how to **banish worry with hope**. Hope is taking action with enthusiasm and not waiting for anyone to solve our problems, looking for the lesson in every situation. Start right NOW to be the person you have always wanted to be, full of hope for the good things to come and the shining star for others to follow. Teach all around you that there is always hope to be better, to find solutions to all problems, to look for better professional options, to improve your health, to have better relations with your loved ones, with your friends and at work.

The only way to find the limits of the possible is by going beyond them to the impossible.
Arthur C. Clarke

2.10 FROM PESSIMISM TO OPTIMISM

How I changed from pessimist to optimist

According to the dictionary, a pessimist is someone who has a tendency to stress the negative things and always takes the gloomiest possible view. During my teenage years I recall worrying too much and exaggerating any negative thing that could happen to me to the level of catastrophe. My friends even gave me a teddy bear of a cartoon figure of a little black chick as a present for my 16th birthday. This little chick was called "Calimero" and he was always worried and only bad things happened to him.

Somewhere along the line I changed and today I am the most fervent optimist. I try to be as realistic as possible but always with that special touch of hope, always trying to see the best side of people and things. I imagine the best possible future and work towards it. I ask myself: **what is the worst possible outcome**? and I am ready to face the consequences. Furthermore, I never forget to take care of the child in me, always trying to be amazed, always trying to find the excitement of adventure, always trying to enjoy the present moment.

I decided that I was going to be the kind of person that says, "When the going gets tough, the tough gets going," when things get really ugly and people start to give up, I am going to stand above the circumstances and get the job done. I think the biggest gift we can give others is to touch each person you meet with a positive spirit and hopefully that person will pass the message on, it is like when you hear someone whistling a song, it is contagious, is it not? And the final question: what does everything mean to you? What is the purpose of life? Are we alone in the universe? I do not know, I only know that it is our decision. Why don't we paint a beautiful picture and enjoy it? By the way, take your diary and write the best possible version of yourself: What would you change to become a real optimist?

"The future belongs to those who believe in the beauty of their dreams."
Eleanor Roosevelt

"I get discouraged now and then when there are clouds of grey,

Until I think about the things that happened yesterday.

I do not mean the day before or those of months ago,

But all the yesterdays in which I had the chance to grow.

I think of opportunities that I allowed to die,

And those I took advantage of before they passed me by.

And I remember that the past presented quite a plight,

But somehow I endured it and the future seemed all right.

And I remind myself that I am capable and free,

And my success and happiness are really up to me."

- **James J. Metcalfe**

3. ACTIONS

What can you do to improve your health, create more wealth and abundance in your life and enjoy it with your loved ones? What actions can you take to create the life of your dreams?

GOD NEPTUNE
Do you want extraordinary results?
Take massive action, persist and you will accomplish more than you could possibly imagine

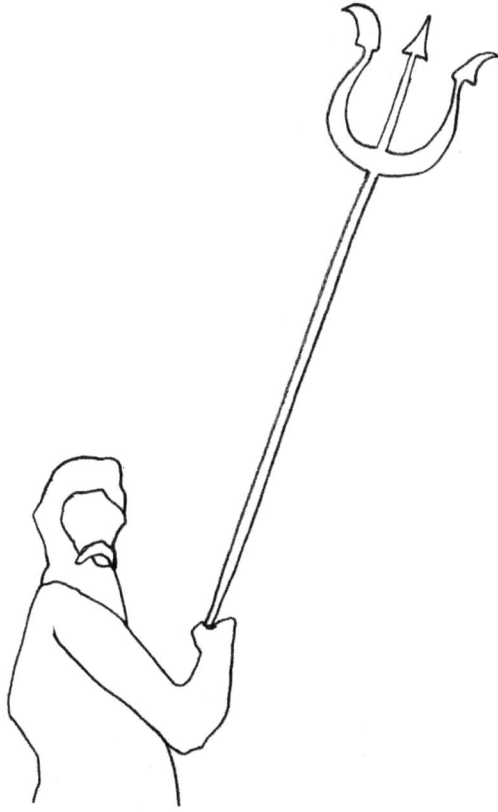

Lord of the seas, earthquakes and horses

1. **How can you improve the mental higher faculties to achieve anything you want and enjoy life?**

From unawareness and emotional ignorance to unlimited power and emotional intelligence

2. **How can you turn your actions into personal virtues?**

From paralysis and procrastination to motivation and virtue

3. **Do you want a long life filled with enriching relationships?**

From poor relationships and health problems to fulfilling relations and a long healthy life

4. **How can you become anything you want and be number one in your profession?**

From average performance to excellence and continuous improvement

5. **How can you develop your wealth and spiritual self?**

From beginner level to expert

3.1 FROM UNAWARENESS TO UNLIMITED POWER

20 years abroad!!!

I have always felt drawn to the field of self-improvement, success and happiness. Since age 17 I have visited two continents, more than fifteen countries and I have visited or lived in more than a hundred cities. I just want to make the point that I have seen quite a lot of human nature, of human desires, of human success and misery. I have seen many people who lost the desire for dreaming and making a difference. Let us make a deal, **why don't we restore the dream together and make it real?**

First, what do you truly want? You can start by raising your standards of what is possible, by changing your beliefs (from why me to how I am going to do it!) and even your strategy (believe and you will find the way). **Second**, you will only produce new results in your life the minute you change your identity. You must change inside to change your world outside. **Third**, the meaning of life is not so much what happens, but the way we interpret and evaluate it and that is done by the questions we ask ourselves, our vocabulary and self-talk.

Get your emotions right. If you are not happy it is because you have certain rules, you do not need anything to feel happy now. Be impeccable in your conduct, what emotional states would you be in if you were at your best on a daily basis?

Be the master of change by associating massive pain to not changing now and massive pleasure to changing now. Make a plan for daily things you can do to gain healthy pleasure. I decided I wanted to contribute in some way that lived on after I was gone, so I wrote this book. If one of the ideas of the book can help you improve your life, I will be more than satisfied.

"**Knowledge itself is power.**"
-Sir Francis Bacon

3.2 FROM EMOTIONAL IGNORANCE TO EMOTIONAL INTELLIGENCE

Emotional ignorance is not knowing what emotions you usually have, how to maximize the positive ones and minimize the negatives ones and, of course, not being able to realize what others are feeling and not knowing how to promote positive relationships. **Let us become emotionally intelligent!**

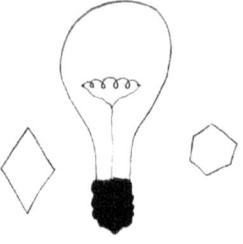

THOUGHTS

1. The motivation behind virtually all behavior is to change the way we feel. So, please choose healthy thoughts and actions.

2. I will give you a magnificent tool bag to change negative to positive emotions: change your physiology (walk quick and straight, shoulders and head up! It is impossible to feel depressed!), change your mental focus, the questions you ask, change your self-talk, your beliefs, your values. You are in command!

3. Be conscious of the consequences of your decisions and actions, identify the negative thoughts and change them.

FEELINGS

4. **Empathy**: understand the feelings and worries of other people. We sometimes are different, we think and feel different.

5. **Intuition**: learn to identify emotional patterns.

6. **Self-acceptance**: feel good about yourself, know your strengths and weaknesses and learn to laugh at yourself.

ACTIONS

7. Develop a plan for emotional control at the beginning of the week. What situations trigger negative emotions? What can you change to produce positive emotions regularly?

8. Be a better communicator: learn to listen, ask and realize the difference between body language and actual words.

9. Assertiveness: express yourself freely in public, enjoy your relationships and add value to other people's lives.

10. Solution of conflicts: learn to negotiate with the model win-win, where both parts benefit from each other.

"**Living with integrity means: Not settling for less than what you know you deserve in your relationships.**"
Barbara De Angelis

3.3 FROM PARALYSIS TO TOTAL MOTIVATION

The door-to-door hero

Bill was born in 1932 in the United States of America with brain damage, which made it difficult for him to talk and walk. The public work agencies and the experts told him he was not fit for work but they did not take into account the force of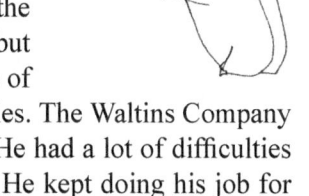
the human spirit. Bill found work in sales. The Waltins Company accepted him in the Portland territory. He had a lot of difficulties even to do the most basic movements. He kept doing his job for 38 years, getting a special award for dedication and commitment at the end.

This story teaches us several wonderful lessons. **Mentally**, the bigger and more significant the goal, the stronger the motivation and drive. Besides, the key to greatness is committed decision that leads to the unstoppable force of persistence. One more powerful weapon to destroy paralysis and create immediate action: **build the most beautiful and vivid image of what you want and hold it in your mind until it becomes reality.**

At the emotional level, all successful and big achievers share several things in common. One of the best ways of enjoying work is having fun doing whatever activity you have chosen to succeed in. Another is to feel what positive psychology has called "**flow,**" meaning, to lose oneself in the task at hand, which creates a high degree of satisfaction and superb results. **Just think how wonderful the world would be if every soul did the same!**

What can one person do? You have the power to create world movements if the cause is right (peace, poverty, environment). Believe in yourself. Make a list of all the advantages of doing the task and all the disadvantages of not doing it. List all the rewards you could give yourself when you succeed. And finally, the real secret to success is taking action and evaluating the results.

"**When the dream is big enough, the facts don´t matter.**"
Sam Kalenuik

3.4 FROM PROCRASTINATION TO VIRTUE

THOUGHTS

1. **Find the fire within yourself.** Successful people love what they do and they feel a strong desire to express the best of their ability. Improve yourself and be more creative every day. Do not compare.

2. The real difference between happy and frustrated individuals is the meaning they decide to give to the circumstances around them. Make the commitment to yourself that nothing will interfere with your level of happiness and then start building on that foundation, with goals, activities and anything you choose.

3. Are your dreams making your life better and are you becoming a better person through them? **Design your own life as a masterpiece,** get rid of all doubts, please.

FEELINGS

4. **Appreciate your gift, it was placed in your heart for you by God** for you to enlighten the world. There is no more enriching pleasure than making a big effort for a noble cause and sharing it with others.

5. The secret to happiness, joy and peace of mind is to follow your heart. It always shows you what makes you feel happy, content, satisfied and in love, and that in turn, makes others happier.

6. We are here to serve, I cannot find a higher purpose.

ACTIONS

7. **Share your gift.** Make a list of your gifts and share it with everyone you see freely on a daily basis, that will make you a happy person.

8. How to face life's problems: The problems in life are not the problem. The secret is to see them as learning experiences to grow.

9. How to face your fears: Take care only of the things you can control and do not worry about the rest. Besides, you do not develop courage if you do not face the fear, so feel the fear and do it anyway.

10. Learn to live with change. It is said that the only certain thing in life is change. Realize that everything is changing; our bodies, our thoughts, our emotions, our relations, our community, our country, our society, our world and our planet.

"Therefore I say unto you. What things soever ye desire, when ye pray, believe that ye receive them, and ye shall have them."
Mark 11:24

3.5 FROM POOR RELATIONS TO FULFILLING RELATIONSHIPS

Nowadays we are witnessing a crisis in relationships. About 50% of couples in the Western World do not make it to the third year after marriage. We will concentrate on romantic relations but the same principles also apply to other relationships.

First, you should know the values and rules of the people with whom you share a relationship. **Second**, see the relationship as a place to give not to get, you do not need anybody to make you feel good. **Third**, make it a priority, you do not want intensity and passion to drift away. **Finally**, remind yourself of what you love about the person, reinforce the feelings of connection and renew your feelings of intimacy and attraction.

Science tells us that the most desired human emotion is the connection with other souls, but unfortunately we are not very skilled at it. As Dr. Barbara DeAngelis explains, there a four pernicious phases that can kill a relationship. Identify and eliminate them before it is too late with clear and honest communication. One, **Resistance**: you are annoyed at something and you do not share it. Two, **Resentment**: you are now angry and an emotional barrier destroys intimacy. Three. **Rejection**: you begin to see everything irritating. Four, **Repression**: you go numb, you avoid feeling either pain or passion and excitement.

Focus each day on making it better and it will become better. Ask your partner what he/she needs to feel loved (see, hear, feel?). For some people it is very important to hear "I love you" every day, whereas other people are more visual and need to see little acts of love (giving flowers, little surprise gifts). Plan one romantic moment a week to keep passion alive and always think: **What can I do today to make this marvelous person happier?** Think: I do not have the right to make this person miserable, she/he loves me!

The people's good is the highest law."
Cicero

3.6 FROM HEALTH PROBLEMS TO A LONG LIFE

THOUGHTS

1. Do the one-week **mental challenge** as often as you need it. For the next seven days refuse to dwell on negative thoughts or feelings. If they come, just let them go. Redirect the focus of your conscious mind to what you want to think, feel and have.

2. Do mental exercises daily, as they reinforce the mental faculties and prevent us from suffering degenerative disorders.

3. Meditate every day at least 5 minutes, your whole being will benefit from it, your mind, your body, your emotions and your soul.

FEELINGS

4. Learn to be happy just because you are alive, then add **a million more things to be happy** about every single day.

5. The secret to health and happiness is to be able to magnify the positive emotions and minimize the negative ones.

6. Feel your heart with the good stuff: love, joy, optimism, playfulness, curiosity, trust, contribution, compassion and passion.

ACTIONS

7. **Nutrition**: Have a king's breakfast, a prince's lunch and a beggar's dinner. Have a balanced and low-calorie diet with carbohydrates, proteins, vitamins, minerals and at least 2 liters of water a day.

8. **Sport**: this is one of the healthiest habits you can ever develop. Do at least half an hour exercise whenever suits you best. The brain produces endorphins, a natural antidepressant. You will love it!

9. **Humor**: smile and laugh as much as you can. Laughing has very positive effects on the immune system. Besides, the person who laughs often is more flexible to any obstacles and influences all the people around with very positive vibrations.

10. **Do as many activities as you can to liberate your soul**, feel free and enchanted with life; dance as if no one is looking, sing as if you were a professional, laugh as if you could not stop and hug others as much as you can, as though you would not see them again.

"A beautiful thing is never perfect."
Proverb

3.7 FROM MEDIOCRITY TO EXCELLENCE

Jim Carrey: from poverty to stardom

Jimmy was a quiet boy with no friends during secondary school in the suburbs of Toronto. He started to do some funny things in the back of the class and realized that his classmates would want to talk to him. Soon he started acting at school and then in a club, but he was quite a failure at that time. His parents were almost poor and had chronic depression. Things were not going very well.

However, he kept doing it over and over again until he succeeded. Even when he was famous, **he kept improving his own style.** When he was in poverty, he kept focused on his dream. He even wrote himself a false check for 10 million dollars for services rendered. When his father died in 1994, he had the real check in his hands. It was the unshakable desire for **raising above poverty** that gave him constant strength.

We can learn from this story that success is many times the **triumph over one self**, knowing that sometimes you have to do the things you do not really feel like doing for a long time. All those who have achieved professional excellence know that there is no time for complaints, that results normally come in the long run and that all you do with enthusiasm and passion will at the end come back multiplied to you.

Many of them, started with nothing, achieved their goals gradually, giving themselves the necessary time for things to evolve, even though they made mistakes along the way, but they knew they would accomplish the dream if the course was maintained.

"Mind is the Master power that molds and makes, And Man is Mind, and evermore he takes the tool of Thought, and shaping what he wills, brings forth a thousand joys or a thousand ills; He thinks in secret and it comes to pass; Environment is but his looking-glass."
James Allen, As A Man Thinketh

3.8 FROM AVERAGE PERFORMANCE TO

CONTINUOUS IMPROVEMENT AT WORK

THOUGHTS

1. What is happiness at work? The mental element is contentment: how the person perceives the realization of specific goals. The affective part is the perception of satisfaction.

2. Be a leader, be an example to others of enthusiasm for the task at hand, always trying to offer a better service to clients, creating better working conditions and higher profit.

3. It is said that we spend more than half our life at the work place; I think we better be as happy as we can there. I invite you to be an example of self-confidence, creativity, success and joy.

FEELINGS

4. Happiness and **team work**: according to several studies, the most effective teams were the ones whose goals were client satisfaction, profit and good work climate.

5. Dealing with **overwhelm**: write down the list of all the things you should do, prioritize, divide the work and the tasks and check progress daily, solving difficulties along the way.

6. Dealing with **boredom**: when routine sets in, it is time to reevaluate the responsibilities, functions and activities of your job or profession. Focus on the ones that make you feel alive, change daily activities and give the rest of task to someone else who can do a good job.

ACTIONS

7. Apply **never-ending improvement** in yourself, your work team and your company. There is always room for improvements.

8. Get involved in coaching or mentoring. It is crucial to be accountable and responsible for your results.

9. Keep working on your strengths and values and it is only a matter of time that new and better opportunities and projects will arrive.

10. Realize where you are professionally, how did you get there? **Set yourself a new goal and apply the same traits.**

"The education and empowerment of women throughout the world cannot fail to result in a more caring, tolerant, just and peaceful life for all."
Aung San Suu Kyi, Nobel Peace Prize

3.9 FROM WEALTH STUDENT TO EXPERT

Though **Andrew Carnegie** proved to be one of the titans of the industrial age,

he was once a poor boy from Scotland. His father was a hand loom weaver, but once the industrialization of society reached Scotland, his father's work was no longer needed. For years, his family had tough times to make ends meet, so they decided to start anew in America. At thirteen, Andrew and his family moved to America and he got a job at a cotton mill. He was working twelve hour days, six days a week. Eventually Andrew got a job as a telegraph messenger. Because of his great work ethic, someone from the Pennsylvania Railroad Company offered him a job, which allowed him to earn more money and make his way up the corporate ladder. He soon started investing in railroad companies, and then hit the jackpot by investing in steel. His investments would allow him to have his own steel company, which was able to bring $120 billion to his wallet.

Rockefeller was born in Richford, New York and was one of six children. His father was a traveling salesman and was a foe of conventional morality. Throughout much of his life, Rockefeller's father tried to find tricks and schemes he could use in order to avoid hard work, or any work at all. John's mom struggled a lot in order to keep stability in the home, especially when her husband was gone for weeks at a time. Rockefeller's family soon moved to Moravia and then to Owego. John went through school and got a job as a bookkeeper where he made about $50 in three months. In 1859, Rockefeller decided to go into business with a friend named Maurice B. Clark. The two established a firm and built an oil refinery. The refinery was run by two other men, but soon after, Rockefeller bought out the Clark bothers' firm, renamed it Rockefeller & Andrews. Soon his brother also bought into the oil business. By the end of it all, Rockefeller was able to found the Standard Oil Company and became the world's first billionaire.

"**Success is following the pattern of life one enjoys more.**"
Al Cappone

3.10 FROM EMPTINESS TO THE MEANING OF LIFE

What is the meaning of life? Good question, probably the most important question in the history of mankind. My personal view, as it must be a personal view, not imposed by anyone, is that life has no meaning, and at the same time, life has many meanings. **It all depends on the meaning you want to give.** After some years, confusion, failures, successes, negative and positive experiences, I can finally say that I know the meaning of my life.

To me, I am a spiritual being in a physical body living in the 21st century on a planet called earth. I love life, being alive and would like to live 100 years. I consider myself to be a happy person and learn everyday to be a bit more fulfilled in all aspects of life. Finally, I would like to be able to share my experiences with others for them to add value to their lives. The more good I do for others, the more fulfilled I feel. Let me share some suggestions:

First, life has more meaning when all the goals you seek are in harmony with each other.

Second, the best way to do this is to have a coherent life plan.

Third, creativity is a great source of meaning to many people.

Next, view any kind of suffering as a learning process.

Furthermore, if you feel it right for you, take advantage of the positive effects of the spiritual and religious experience.

Finally, make it a habit to develop hope and optimism. Just try to deepen your knowledge and sense of meaning every day. It is a fascinating journey!

"To laugh is to risk appearing the fool. To weep is to risk appearing sentimental. To reach out for another is to risk involvement. To expose feelings is to risk exposing your true self. To place your ideas before a crowd is to risk their loss. To love is to risk not being loved in return. To live is to risk dying. To hope is to risk despair. To try is to risk failure."

-Author unknown

4. INDIVIDUAL BEING
Who do you want to be?

GOD VULCAN
**Act as the person you want to be,
You will become it as surely as night follows day**

**Master blacksmith and craftsman of the gods;
god of fire and the forge**

1. **Do you want to master the art of self-control?**

From chaos and lack or order to organization and self-control

2. **How can you exercise the power of determination?**

From laziness and immaturity to determination and maturity

3. **How to develop social responsibility and moderation as guiding principles in your life?**

From lack of social engagement and excess in different areas to responsibility and moderation

4. **Do you know how much you can achieve with persistence?**

From irregular effort and apathy to persistence and hard work

5. **How to become financial independent and just?**

From lack of financial control and injustice to financial independence and justice

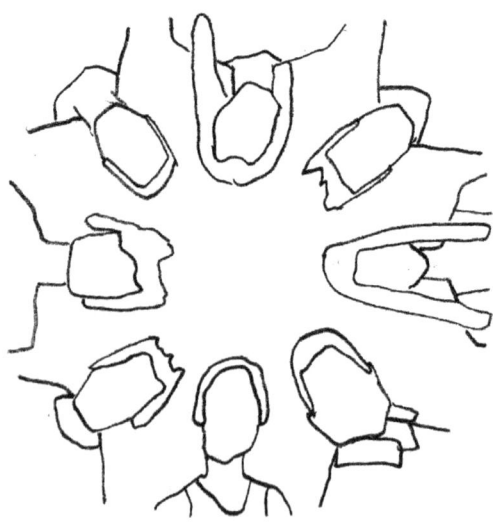

4.1 FROM CHAOS TO ORDER

How I left the land of confusion!

I believe life is a never-ending learning process and we very often feel lost and confused. I have been there but thanks God I gained clarity and order in my life. There are many ways to live life. One common denominator to all human beings is the search for security in all areas. A tendency is to use one of those areas as our anchor to **security**; the problem is however, that we live in a constant emotional rollercoaster, reacting to the different events of that specific area.

A better and more intelligent way of living is being focused on **eternal principles**. They do not go crazy or start treating us in a different way. They do not get divorced or are unfaithful. They are safe from fire, earthquakes and robberies. They are fundamental and crucial guiding lines in life. In this book I made a summary of human values to a hundred. Depending on the author, from modern to ancient times, they mentioned love as the main principle to more than a hundred. So, dear friend, from now on you do not have to hold on to anything with fear, you have 100 new friends by your side all the time. Just let them get in your life, and think, feel and act with and through them.

Partner. Just let love guide you and be understanding.

Family. We should not use love to condition our family members, we should just love every one of them unconditionally.

Possessions. My priority is being and loving, not having.

Work. I take steps to have balance in all areas of my life.

Pleasure. Meaning is much greater than superficial pleasures.

Friends or foes. You decide what the events mean to you.

Church. I am aware of the goodness in all world religions.

One self. From selfishness to continuous growth.

"The high minded man must care more for the truth than for what people think."
Aristotle

4.2 FROM LACK OF ORDER TO SELF-CONTROL

Growing is a process we do as we walk through life, based mainly on two pillars, self-knowledge and self-control. One the one hand, knowing oneself was one the highest values in ancient Greek culture. It is crucial in an increasingly demanding society, bombarded by thousand different messages. It allows us to value our talents and abilities and do the journey with optimism. On the other hand, Self-control is wisdom.

THOUGHTS

1. **Know yourself first**. Ask yourself what you want, how you want to be, the reasons why you are not getting the results you want and what is your action plan to change the situation.

2. Develop **mental control** that leads to calmness and serenity.

3. Tell yourself: "Every day I have a better control of myself."

FEELINGS

4. **Calmness**. Once you feel calm and optimistic, you can think and evaluate whatever challenge life is throwing at you.

5. Eliminate impulsive reactions by counting from 0 to 10.

6. Congratulate and reward yourself for your self-control.

ACTIONS

7. Do this **morning routine**: take a few minutes to relax, breathe deeply and clear your mind of any thought. Just think ONE.

8. Make a list of the difficult situations and have a clear picture in your mind of yourself enjoying the situation being solved!

9. Use **Conscious Tension Control Technique**. After doing you relaxation, think in macros of three elements and do in micro. For example: right after getting up, I do my exercises, have a shower and get dressed. In each of the areas you enjoy the task. When you finish, you have a very powerful sense of tranquility and accomplishment. Then another set of 3 macros.

10. Use the **Rational Emotive Therapy**. You question the thoughts that produce negative emotions by saying: "It is not true that this event always happens. It might take place sometimes but I have the power to change the situation or how I think about it."

"Courage is the price that Life exacts for granting peace."
Amelia Earhart

4.3 FROM LAZINESS TO PERSISTENCE

Napoleon Hill (1883-1970) was an American author and one of the earliest producers of the modern genre of personal-success literature. His most famous work, *Think and Grow Rich*, is one of the best-selling books of all time (at the time of Hill's death in 1970, *Think and Grow Rich* had sold 20 million copies). Hill's works examined the power of personal beliefs and the role they play in personal success. He became an advisor to President Franklin D. Roosevelt from 1933-36.

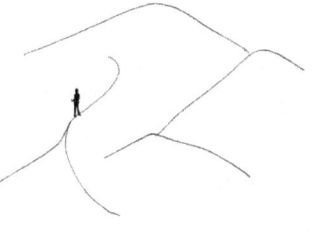

The majority of people are ready to give up their aims and

desires when opposition or difficulties arrive. A few carry on despite all opposition until they produce the desired results. These are the Fords, Carnegies, Rockefellers and Edisons.

As Hill used to say, persistence is a state of mind and it can be cultivated by mastering the following areas:

1. **Definiteness of purpose.** A strong motive forces one to face any challenges in life, regardless of the level of difficulty.

2. **Desire.** The stronger the desire, the easier it is to keep up.

3. **Self-reliance.** Develop your ability to follow your dream.

4. **Definiteness of plans.** Organize, prioritize and review progress.

5. **Accurate knowledge.** This eliminates uncertainty and anxiety.

6. **Co-operation.** Create a team with understanding and sympathy.

7. **Will-power.** The power of concentration makes wonders.

8. **Habit.** Repetition is the key to forming healthy habits.

9. **Apply** these principles and qualities to your life and make it a habit. They are essential for success in all walks of life.

10. **Results.** This is the sweet reward for all who learn to take the steps. They will lead you to your economic desires, freedom and independence of thought, power and fame; they transform dreams into physical realities and they also lead to the mastery of fear, discouragement and indifference.

"What the mind of man can conceive and believe, it can achieve."
Napoleon Hill

4.4 FROM IMMATURITY TO MATURITY

According to **Steven R. Covey**, author of the international bestseller *The Seven Habits of Highly Effective People*, maturity is a process of going from being dependent, independent to interdependent. That is, from depending on things and everybody else to make us happy, to becoming an independent individual, and finally, realizing we are all interdependent with each other.

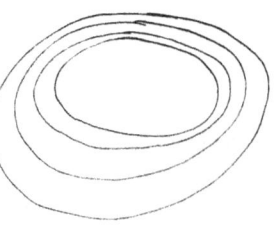

THOUGHTS

1. Think in win-win situations. When we balance our wants with other people's needs, we are laying the foundation for better relationships, a better society and the common good.

2. Start with a goal in mind gives us the certainty, security and serenity of knowing where we are going and what we want. You cannot reach any port if you do not know **your destination**.

3. First things first. Learn to differentiate between urgent and **important** aspects and live your life dealing with important issues. This will give you vision, balance, discipline and control.

FEELINGS

4. Be proactive means being responsible for your actions and being free to respond to life's situation as we wish, becoming the co-creators of our lives, as opposed to be in constant reaction.

5. First **understand others** before you try others to understand you. It is one of the most intense desires human beings have. Learn the skill and your relationships will improve immediately.

6. Find synergy. It is the synthesis of different views that produce better and superior ideas based on team work.

ACTIONS

7. Apply being proactive to a specific problem for a week.

8. Write your personal mission in life, most important goals.

9. Change your time distribution according to your needs.

10. Apply the principle of empathy to a given relationship.

"Sometimes questions are more important than answers."
Nancy Willard, American poet

4.5 FROM LACK OF SOCIAL ENGAGEMENT TO RESPONSIBILITY & LEADERSHIP

You saved my career!

A man called Bob ran towards the well-known speaker **John C. Maxwell** once and said: "You saved my career!" I am so grateful. Then Mr. Maxwell asked: "How did I do that?" The man answered: "I am fifty-three years old and I have been in a position of leadership for the last seventeen years but I struggled so much due to my lack of leadership. Last year I went to one of your seminars, applied what I learned and now the team acknowledges me as a great leader. **Thank you for having made a leader out of me!**"

Let us see how to improve our abilities to become better leaders:

THOUGHTS

1. **Influence**. The main purpose is to have followers. Understand the most important aspects of your followers and yourself.

2. **Priorities**. Success is the realization of a worthy ideal. Please, differentiate between important aspects and the details.

3. **Vision**. Be passionate about the goal first to persuade others to follow you. What you see is what you will end up achieving.

FEELINGS

4. **Attitude**. This is the most important aspect in life.

5. **People**. The more people you teach, the greater your work.

6. Make a positive change but start with **yourself** as example.

ACTIONS

7. **Integrity** is the correlation between your words and your actions. People will do what you do, not what you tell them to do.

8. Solve **potential problems** before they become emergencies. Please, tell your team what, how and why they should do it.

9. **Self-discipline**. This is the most important asset. You will produce the most powerful impact by who you are!

10. **Personal development**. Create the proper environment and both your team and you will grow exponentially.

"You were not born a winner, and you were not born a loser. You are what you make yourself be."
Lou Holtz

4.6 FROM EXCESS TO MODERATION & WELL-BEING

THOUGHTS

1. Live according to your **aspirations** not your basic needs. Your aspirations include everything you want to achieve in life, whereas your inclinations include all the past old habits. Practice being your best self.

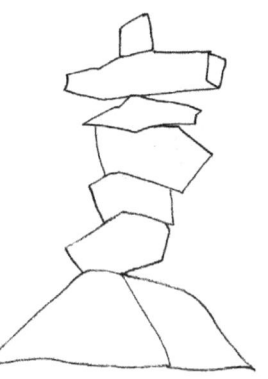

2. Attain and maintain your **optimal state**. How do you feel when you are happy? Remember it and produce the feeling whenever you want. People say they feel eager, energized, alert, relaxed and enthusiastic. They also feel powerful, free of tension and focused.

3. Command your well-being. Good food, regular exercise and adequate sleep are crucial to happiness, effectiveness and well-being. Avoid foods that make you feel good for a few minutes and feel badly for hours.

FEELINGS

4. **Tension** inhibits happiness. Stop strangling yourself with stress. Happiness is radiant, relaxed, joyous, confident and free.

5. Triumph over **anxiety**. The best antidote is a great big belly laugh. Try it, laugh out loud for no reason. Get going with a giggle. You will feel better and make others happier, too.

6. Cast off **tension**. See yourself smiling, successful and feeling great in your mind's eye. Practice this until it becomes a habit.

ACTIONS

7. Take **breathing** breaks. Breath is life. To be happy, breathe easily, deeply and well. Use a breathing break whenever you need it.

8. Relaxed well-being requires **balance** and breathing. To feel happy and confident, balance your body upright, breathe deeply and radiate relaxed and energized well-being.

9. **Radiate energy**. Focus on how you want to feel. Feel good feelings, project them. They can become genuinely yours.

10. Eliminate **negativity**, fear, anger and all negative emotions. Ask yourself: What am I thinking right now? I do not have any evidence to think and feel that way. Everything will be just fine, God is with me!

"Knowledge is love and light and vision."
Helen Keller

4.7 FROM IRREGULAR EFFORT TO DETERMINATION

How I learned the German language

It is funny how things work sometimes and how confusing other people's comments can be. The first foreign language I learned was English. We had it in school but I was a disaster. It wasn't until I spent one year in an English-speaking country that I really learned. When I was 19 years old I decided to go to London, England, and earned a degree in Applied Language Studies for four years. My third language was German.

I had two great experiences. The first one was public speaking. We used to talk in front of the class twice a week in different languages about any possible topic. As teachers told us: "You will hate speaking in public but at the end of four years, you are going to love it!" Guess what? They were right. You end up loving being able to communicate, to **inspire** and maintain people's attention.

The other experience was learning that difficult language, German. I spent one year studying vocabulary, grammar, listening to news, reading papers and giving talks. I remember the head teacher of the German department saying to me one time in front of the class: "Oscar, you are not good in languages, you will never learn German!" Wow, what an inspirational comment that was, **I was really ashamed**! However, I did not let anything stand in the way of my resolution. I was going to work as a translator and interpreter in Spanish, English and German. After the degree in London, I spent four years in Germany. The best compliment I have ever received in languages has been both in England and Germany, just talking to people in different situations. They thought I was an English man in England and German in Germany. I think I reached a good level of performance in the languages, did I not?

"Just forget what others say about you. Persistence is your best friend and will perform miracles in your life."
Oscar Escallada

4.8 FROM APATHY TO SELF-REALIZATION

Self-realization is a concept that has become widely popular in the Western World. It has been greatly influenced by some Eastern religions. For instance, for the Hindu religion self-realization refers to a profound spiritual awakening where there is an awakening from an illusory self identify image (Ego), to the true, divine, perfect condition that the individual is. The branch of Advaita Vedanta is the one that has especially developed this concept.

Also, **Abraham Maslow** and **Carl Rogers**, American psychologists, developed the concept of **self-actualization** in Humanistic Psychology. Maslow defined then self-realization as "the impulse to convert oneself into what one is **capable of being**."

Based on Maslow, the most common meaning given to self-realization is that of psychological growth and maturation. It represents the awakening and manifestation of latent potentialities of the human being. Let us see the most important traits of self-realization:

THOUGHTS

1. Truth: honesty with yourself and others.

2. Self-acceptance.

3. Self-sufficiency, autonomy, independence and self-determination.

FEELINGS

4. Goodness, rightness and simplicity.

5. Aliveness and spontaneity.

6. Fulfillment, being pleased with different life's areas.

ACTIONS

7. Be unique and proud of your individuality.

8. Justice, fairness and non-partiality.

9. Convince yourself that you can do things with ease.

10. Playfulness, fun, joy and amusement.

"Wonder is the beginning of wisdom."
Greek Proverb

4.9 FROM LACK OF FINANCIAL CONTROL TO FINANCIAL INDEPENDENCE

Killing The Goose That Laid the Golden Eggs!

A cottager and his wife had a hen that laid a golden egg every day. They supposed that the hen must contain a great lump of gold in its inside, and in order to get the gold they killed it. Having done so, they found to their surprise that the hen differed in no respect from their other hens. The foolish pair, thus hoping to become rich all at once, deprived themselves of the gain of which they were assured day by day. This fable teaches us the danger of being **greedy**, wanting more than we really need. There are many paths or theories to financial freedom, that is, not having to work to be able to cover life's expenses. Let me illustrate just a general idea. I advise you to become your own expert, it is a phenomenal experience.

1. **Slow-and-Steady Conventional Path.** A regular job can give you a regular income and security, at least in the first stages.

2. **The Mind-Over-Matter Motivational Path.** Determine

how best to mix the motivational (self-help books) and the practical (more technical material) and determine which works best for you.

3. **Robert Kiyosaki**, author. He teaches that you can make your own rules, especially in this society of rapid change.

4. **The Middle-Class Worker's Path**. Amy Dacyczyn explains how to live on low incomes and how to make powerful changes.

5. **The Intelligent Idealist's Path**. Joe Dominguez gives a lot of ideas on how to retire early with financial freedom.

6. **The Dweller's Path**. John Greaney leads a movement on negativity. It is always good to know what not to do.

7. **The Non-Consumerist DINK's Path** (Paul Terhorst), mainly for married couples with double income and no kids. The idea is to trade expensive possessions for the freedom of not working.

8. **The Holistic Soul-Searcher's Path**. This is about taking many ideas from different sources, being conservative and flexible at the same time and taking small steps to a great financial future.

"**Plan your financial future, you plan life.**"
Oscar Escallada

4.10 FROM LACK OF FAITH TO RELIGION AND SPIRITUALITY

Science cannot overlook the fact that spirituality and religion have a very powerful and positive influence in our lives, in our health, well-being, relationships and happiness. Only in the United States the majority of people believe in God. If you decide it can enrich your life, you can take advantage of the benefits for your life and happiness.

I am a spiritual and religious person. It makes a lot of sense to me and helps me a lot with **life's challenges**.

Spirituality is the search of the sacred, the meaning of life through something bigger than oneself. Spiritual people refer to God as divine power or supreme truth. Religion also presupposes a spiritual search but in a more formal and institutionalized way. Some people are only spiritual, some are both religious and spiritual and some are neither of them. According to scientific studies, spiritual/religious people have better mental and physical health, cope with stress better, have happier marriages, consume drugs and alcohol less frequently and live longer.

I strongly recommend to deepen your understanding and knowledge of spirituality and religion for the following reasons:

1. General meaning of life and negative events.

2. Spiritual strength in difficult times (disease, death, unemployment).

3. Sense of control of our destiny and personal situations.

4. Feelings of hope, gratitude, love, compassion and joy.

5. Positive emotions and experiences related to happiness.

6. Happier marriage and family life.

7. Social support and the sense of belonging to a supporting community that offers help, friendship and companionship increases self-esteem and identity (church, temple).

8. Have better mental and physical health.

9. Lead a more positive and less stressful lifestyle.

10. Prayer, meditation and reading spiritual literature is an excellent way of developing spirituality in our lives every day.

"If you judge people, you have no time to love them."
Mother Theresa, social worker

5. SOCIAL BEING
What type of social relations do you want to have?

GODDESS VESTA

Be an example of love and support to others, uncountable blessings will surely descend upon you

Goddess of the hearth and of the right ordering of domesticity and the family

1. What relationship do you want to have with yourself

and with your parents?

From personal unawareness and unfulfilling relationships to self-knowledge and gratitude

2. **How can you be a better brother/sister and friend?**

From family conflicts and resentment to understanding and loyalty

3. **How can you improve your relationship with your partner and your work colleagues?**

From "love" with conditions and the average employee mentality to unconditional love and being your number one

4. **Do you want to be happy and fulfilled parents and grandparents?**

From neglect and inexperience to care and wisdom

5. **Would you like to improve your connection with your community and the world?**

From lack of social concern and individuality to responsibility as a social leader and the serenity of oneness with humanity

MY OWN SELF

5.1 FROM PERSONAL UNAWARENESS TO SELF-KNOWLEDGE

I am already 40 years old and I have already had quite a few experiences in life. I have lived in different countries, studied two bachelor's degrees and three master's degrees, worked in several different countries and managed to become hotel manager. It has been an interesting process of self-discovery. I have traveled a lot but the most interesting journey was the one I made in the discovery of **who I am**, my talents, my weaknesses, and above all, my passions. Let me make a short summary of interesting points to bear in mind:

A clear mind is where all starts. **First**, keep your ideas and dreams to yourself. Let people ask you and wonder by your results and the happiness you radiate. **Second**, read, talk to experts, but believe in yourself, when it comes to your life's decisions. **Third**, think for yourself. We are all vulnerable inside. We all have fears and concerns. We all want to be loved and accepted. Please, make sure you know what you want, do your thinking and do your research.

In the **emotional arena**, I learned that it is ok to feel negative emotions. Let them out, deal with them and get on with things. Besides, true happiness comes from within and the best thing is not to make it conditional to anything or anyone. Please, try to find or create an environment where you can be yourself and reminds you what is important in life.

Important things **to do**? Always find time for yourself, look after your mind, body and emotions, demand respect and be part of the solutions of this world and not of the problems.

> "It is one of the beautiful compensations of this life that no one can sincerely try to help another without helping himself."
> **Charles Dudley Warner**

TO SONS & DAUGHTERS

5.2 FROM UNFULLFILLING RELATIONSHIPS TO CHILDREN'S LOVE

This part is dedicated to all of you in the role of a son or a daughter. I think our parents deserve the best in the world, don't you? They gave us life, loved us and gave us everything, so that we could be happy. Why not try to be a better son or daughter every day regardless of age?

Any regrets, resentment, conflicts? Just let it be, **forgiveness** is the antidote. Erase any bad feelings towards others or yourself. Your life starts right now and you are going to have a phenomenal experience!

THOUGHTS

1. Know what they like. Each person has their own style, feelings and hobbies.

2. Express your appreciation for all that your parents have done for you. Don't take anything for granted and show them your gratitude.

3. Look for common activities you can all share and enjoy.

FEELINGS

4. Be honest. Don't lie to them. Help them to build a wall of trust for you, but when you get it, don't let it fall down again!

5. Be independent and take good care of yourself. Be mature and try not to have them worry about you all the time.

6. Love, help and be kind to your brothers and sisters, be the one who solves conflicts. It is not your business if others do not help.

ACTIONS

7. Try your best at school, university, sports, work. That is going to be good for you, your mates, your brothers and sisters, your parents, your friends and all people you come in contact with.

8. Help them with the housework if you live with them. If not, be in contact with them and help them in any way you possibly can.

9. Do not be shy about showing your love to your parents. Do it in the best way they would understand it (words, actions, gifts).

10. Keep your sense of humor. As in many relationships, if you can laugh together, you are doing okay already.

"Pure love is a willingness to give without a thought of receiving anything in return."
Peace Pilgrim, pacifist

TO BROTHERS & SISTERS

5.3 FROM FAMILY CONFLICTS TO UNDERSTANDING YOUR BROTHERS & SISTERS

Two brothers lived on two sides of a mountain. One was rich but had no children, the other had many children but was very poor. The rich brother thought, I have so much and my brother has so little, let me secretly cross the mountain in the middle of the night and bring my brother extra crop. The poor brother said, I derive so much happiness from my children, let me secretly bring my brother some of my crop so he could have a little extra joy.

And so it went every night each of the brothers secretly crossed the mountain to bring his brother food. Every morning the brothers would inspect their stock to learn nothing was missing. Neither could explain the phenomena but they thanked God for his kindness and continued in their good will.

After years of this routine a schedule change occurred. Instead of the two brothers missing each other in the night, there on top of the mountain the two brothers met. They looked at each other in surprise and then simultaneously realized what had been happening for all the years. They both spontaneously embraced one another, there on top of the mountain as they cried. Who these two brothers were we do not know, but it was on that mountain top, the legend goes, a Holy Temple was built, honoring the love between brothers and sisters.

Marvelous story! We can also do many things: Tell your siblings how you feel, offer to watch your nieces and nephews. Make time for them. Set a good example. Offer advice and a shoulder to cry on. Help them when they need a helping hand. Spend time with your parents. Be the brother/sister who visits your parents and helps with family issues. Finally, develop loyalty, respect, trust, reliability and sense of humor.

"Generosity is giving more than you can, and pride is taking less than you need."
Kahlil Gibran

FRIENDS

5.4 FROM RESENTMENT TO LOYALTY BETWEEN FRIENDS

THOUGHTS

1. The greatest secret to treat people is "make them **feel important.**" It is the deepest human need. If you can do that, you will be loved by everyone.

2. You can always become a very pleasant person: have a **sincere interest** in others, smile, remember people's names, be a good listener, talk about people's interests.

3. You can conquer your enemies. Show **respect** for other people's opinions. Try to avoid saying the other person is wrong.

FEELINGS

4. The best way of dealing with **complaints** is let the other person do the talking. You listen attentively, say you understand the feeling of frustration and say you will do everything to solve the problem.

5. Make other people feel **comfortable** with what you want. Be honest and empathic, and show them the benefits of the action to take.

6. How can you criticize and not be hated? You can do it but in an indirect way. Praise the person and **suggest** another action!

ACTIONS

7. Those who can do this, have the world at their feet. **Motivate** them. Wake them up, create a worthy ideal in their minds and hearts.

8. Allow others to **look good** in front of other people.

9. How can you motivate for success? Praise any positive step towards success. Be generous in praise.

10. What everybody wants is to feel their ideas are important. Avoid arguments, show respect for other people's ideas, acknowledge your mistakes, make people believe in what you want them to do, make them feel as though the idea belongs to them and be **kind**.

"Those who don't know how to weep with their whole heart don't know how to laugh."
Golda Meir, first female Prime Minister of Israel

LOVERS

5.5 UNCONDITIONAL LOVE

The most important thing in life is what to live for and who to live for. Two life projects in one.

There was this guy who believed very much in true love and decided to take his time to wait for his right girl to appear. He believed that there would definitely be someone special out there for him, but none came. Every year at Christmas, his ex-girlfriend would return from Canada to look him up. He was aware that she still held some hope of re-kindling the past romance with him. He did not wish to mislead her in any way. Hence, he would always get one of his girl friends to pose as his girlfriend whenever she came back.

One day he went to his friend's party alone.

"Hey, how come you are all alone this year? Where are all your girlfriends? What happened to that Canadian babe who joins you every Christmas?" asked one of his friends. He thought for a while and finally realized that he had already found his dream girl and she was the Canadian girl all along! It was not any specific girl he was seeking! It was perfection that he wanted!

He then decided to phone the girl, only to learn from her father that she had passed away in a car accident. The guy was devastated. How he hated himself for taking so long to realize his mistake!

Treasure what you have.

Time is too slow for those who wait;

Too swift for those who fear;

Too long for those who grief;

Too short for those who rejoice;

But for those who love...

Time is Eternity.

For all of you out there with someone special in your heart, cherish that person. Cherish every moment that you spend together with that special someone, for in life, anything can happen anytime. You may painfully regret only to realize that it is too late!

AT WORK

5.6 FROM AVERAGE EMPLOYEE MENTALITY TO BEING YOUR NUMBER ONE

THOUGHTS

1. Be a **rock star**. Be the best you can be at work, in your performance and with your mates.

2. Think like an **executive**. Make the success of your company your responsibility. Increase sales, reduce costs and improve benefits.

3. **Learn** more to earn more. The best investment you can do is to develop your abilities and increase your value.

FEELINGS

4. **Be a happy person**! The happier you are, the higher blessing you will be for those around you. It is simple. Do more things that make you happy. Plan them in your daily routine and do them.

5. Be **overenthusiastic**! Enjoy everything. Regard changes as opportunities for growth, love and live with passion.

6. Inspire others to be **great**! Greatness arrives in your life when you are able to inspire others to do great things, too.

ACTIONS

7. **Work hard** and get lucky. Successful people work harder

than those around them. Become excellent in your profession, work smart and hard and be passionate about what you do. Have your working space as tidy and organized as possible, it says a lot about you.

8. Learn to **say no**. Every time you say yes to unimportant things, you are saying no to important things.

9. **Relax**, have fun and be more productive. It has been proven that the best ideas come when you are relaxed and enjoying your work.

10. Have **superb relations** with workmates. Respect everybody, be positive, open and honest, say "please" and " thank you", promise less and do more, leave people better than you found them, be kind and generous, improve your listening ability, become passionate about people and smile often. Try to know as many workmates in your company as possible and greet them every day.

"How wonderful it is that nobody need wait a single moment before starting to improve the world."
Anne Frank, writer

COMMUNITY LEADERSHIP

5.7 FROM LACK OF SOCIAL CONCERN TO RESPONSIBILITY AS A SOCIAL LEADER

Dear reader, I did not use to be very involved in social matters, but the older I get, the more I realized that we are all connected, we are all a big family on a spinning planet in a very subtle biochemical balance, probably alone in the galaxy. So, I think we should all help each other as much as we can and the best way is by being a good citizen. Let see some things we can do:

1. Help Out. You can help out in almost any way. It's all up to you. What do you do best? Do you have a green thumb?

If so, then you can plant at your community garden. Do you have a lot of clothes in your closet that you don't wear anymore? Give them to charity!

2. Be kind. You can't give people dirty looks and be rude if you want to be a good citizen. Smile and treat everyone with respect.

3. Be an example. Pick up litter if you see trash laying around don't just stare at it and walk pass it.

4. Your Encouragement helps even if you are just encouraging the little seven-year-old down the street to learn to ride a bicycle.

5. Have Good Judgment. Don't do anything that would ruin a reputation

6. Donate. Once again, this can be done in so many ways.

7. Be polite. Say "Please" and "Thank You."

8. Be helpful. Smile a lot. Do stuff other people wouldn't.

9. Be a good citizen not because you want an award; rather, act like a citizen every day and you will become comfortable with doing it.

10. Study social and political affairs and get involved in community work, you could even start a career in politics!.

"Any labor that uplifts humanity has dignity and importance and should be undertaken with painstaking excellence."
Martin Luther King, Jr.

PARENTS

5.8 FROM NEGLECT TO CARE

Being a parent is one of the most fulfilling experiences a person can have. The most important thing however, that any parent can give their child, is a sense of being loved. But remember: **You don't have to be infallible to be a "perfect" parent.**

THOUGHTS

1. Be a **model** of healthy living for them. They will do what their parents do, not what they tell them to do. Talk to them about important issues such as drugs, alcohol, sex and the world.

2. Be **consistent**. Enforce rules that apply to every person leading a happy and productive life, not model rules of your ideal/dream person.

3. Always be their **guide** but allow them to live their lives. Let them make mistakes and learn from the experience, avoid criticism.

FEELINGS

4. **Express** love and affection. Tell them you love them every day. Give them lots of hugs and kisses. Boost their confidence with encouragement, appreciation and approval. Love unconditionally.

5. Help them feel **safe**. Respect their privacy as you would want them to respect yours. Do not argue in front of the children!. It only makes them insecure and fearful.

6. **Praise** your children and make them feel special and unique. Teach them that it is fine to be different and that everyone has a gift.

ACTIONS

7. **Listen** to them. Really listen to their concerns and worries.

8. Provide **order**. Set boundaries such as bedtimes and curfews, so they learn that they have limitations. By doing so, they actually get a sense of being loved and cared about by their parents.

9. Give up your **vices**: gambling, alcohol and drugs can jeopardize your child's security. Smoking almost always introduces health hazards to your child's environment.

10. Spend a lot of **time** with them and love them with all your heart, but don't stifle/smother them.

"When you find peace within yourself, you become the kind of person who can live at peace with others."
Peace Pilgrim, spiritual leader

GRANDPARENTS

5.9 FROM INEXPERIENCE TO WISDOM

The following is a fiction letter of a little kid to his grandparents:

Dear Grandma and Grandpa,

I love to hear your **wise advice**. Sorry if sometimes it looks like I am not listening, but in reality I am all ears!

I also like when you give advice to mom and dad. Sometimes I overhear them saying that they have some problems.

Thank you for **taking care** of me, for knowing what I like and for asking me what I think about a lot of things.

I am especially fascinated by the **stories** of your days and love it when you read to me books for us, for children.

Wow! The gifts, the **gifts**, those are my favorite!

I love pictures. I love to see **pictures** with all of us in them. I love seeing mom and dad when they were little, too.

I want to **be** with you every day! I know you have your own house, but... why don't you come every day?

Did my parents really do that when they were younger? I have to tell mom. Did they really have those old **toys**?

A boy in school has a new toy, it's cool! Can you tell mom and dad to buy it? I want to play with you. I want to make a cake or cookies with you. Can you **teach** me some games?

Shall we go to the beach or to the park tomorrow? or better to the river, well... I want to go to the cinema, too. Well, I don't know, but please come and let's do something together!

Dear Grandma and Grandpa, you do so many things for me and I don't know what I do for you, but I promise you one thing, I love you and I will always love you!

"How far you go in life depends on your being tender with the young, compassionate with the aged, sympathetic with the striving and tolerant of the weak and strong. Because someday in your life you will have been all of these."
George Washington.

ONENESS WITH HUMANITY

5.10 FROM INDIVIDUALITY TO THE SERENITY OF ONENESS WITH HUMANITY

In my case, I have learned to love myself, my fellowmen and women for what they are and I love this adventure called life. I do my morning ritual, that is, I express gratitude to God for all that I have in my life, ask that everything works out fine not only in my life but also in the life of those who I love. Then I do some short meditation and visualization of my dreams, and my physical exercises. It does not take that long, about fifteen minutes. So, when I have my thoughts, feelings and soul all set, then I go about my daily activities. I do all of them with passion and joy.

Self-love. Accept yourself for what you are, for your self-esteem, your talents and abilities, your capacity to make decisions and for the conviction that you love yourself and you are your best friend.

Love to your fellowmen and women. This is the love you have for other people. Feel the affection other people have for you, be a good person to be with and take care of your friends and loved ones.

Love for life. Love and take care of your profession, enjoy the daily activities and the little things, develop your social skills, learn how to live, face life's challenges with optimism, and above all, enjoy every single minute you are given.

Look for the **connection** with your higher power. The spirit is that energy that is bigger than you. The more you experience that connection, the more magical life becomes. You can pray, sit in silence, listen to inspirational music or walk in nature.

The power of prayer. I find it very important to pray as you maintain the connection with the higher self. As for religion, there are many.

Light meditation. Concentrate on a mantra and repeat it.

Listen to your inner voice. Ask a question, answer without thinking and then act on it, that is your inner wisdom!. Trust God, let go!.

"We are spiritual beings, connect with it!"
Oscar Escallada

6. HEALTH

How can you have extraordinary health and feel full of energy all the time?

GODDESS HYGEIA

As you treat your body the first half of your life, so will it treat you the second half

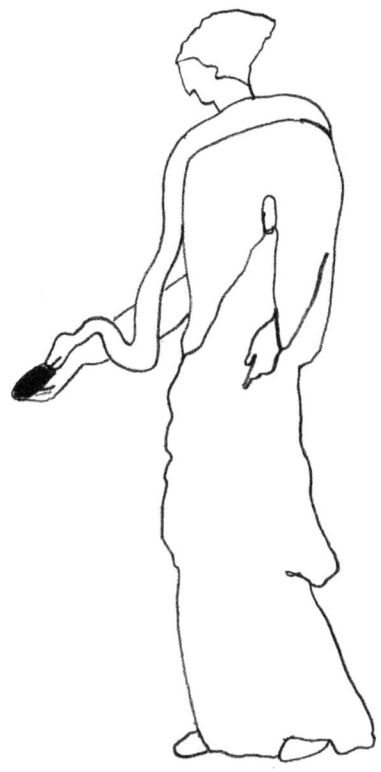

Goddess of health

1. **How can you have a perfect mental health?**

From mental weakness and distress to mental hygiene and harmony between the body and the mind

2. **How can you multiply your emotional intelligence?**

From emotional hardship and ignorance to emotional intelligence and stability of character

3. **How do you enjoy a long healthy life with a spectacular body?**

From disease and an unhealthy lifestyle to a long happy life and loads of vitality and energy

4. **Would you like to improve your relation to family and friends?**

From broken families and loneliness to happy families and fulfilling relationships

5. **What does your ideal professional life look like?**

From an unbalanced life and a sense of being lost to balance family-work and personal definition of ambition

MENTAL

6.1 FROM MENTAL WEAKNESS TO MENTAL HYGIENE

So your body is fit, but there's still that piece of your mind that isn't quite right. Bad mental hygiene creates many problems; settle things. It may be that you need to get your head straight. It's easy to improve your mental health, and you've already taken the first step by looking into it. Remember, it all starts from within. These are some of the things I keep in mind and do. I hope they are helpful to you:

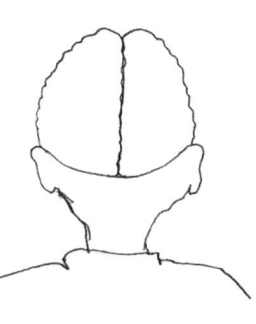

1. **Feed your mind.** Improve your social relations, and allow for more warmth and love between the people closest to you.

2. **Challenge yourself** once in a while. Seek a meaningful job to obtain a sense of real self-worth and confidence or focus on the positive and interesting aspects of your present position.

3. Fill your mind with your personal **"mental food"** (optimism). You will experience less boredom and inner conflict.

4. **Surround yourself** with beauty. Redecorate your house or garden. Do some spring cleaning. Put on some happy music.

5. Be sure to **identify** any issues you have such as anxiety or other disorders. Identify them, deal with them or seek help.

6. Accept yourself, forgive yourself and carry on. Do you have some feelings of guilt for past **failures**? They were not really failures but important lessons to learn from.

7. Develop a **hobby** or passion for your mind to express your emotions and joys to feel progress.

8. Recover old **friendships**, or make new true friendships to feed that part of your mind. Have a good social support system.

9. Make sure you're consuming a balanced and healthy **diet** with the right vitamins and minerals every day.

10. Make the most out of the **present moment**, be patient and flexible, and be open to new possibilities and to other people.

"If you plan on being anything less than you are capable of being, you will probably be unhappy all the days of your life."
Abraham Maslow

6.2 FROM DISTRESS TO HARMONY BETWEEN THE BODY AND THE MIND

THOUGHTS

1. Make it a **way of life**. Once taught, your mind will be the generator of positive thoughts, happy feelings, effective actions and spectacular results in your life.

2. Use **common sense** and make mature decisions. Gather up information, take your time, decide and act.

3. **Reason objectively**. The balanced person sees things in an objective way, looks for the causes and tries to find the best possible solution.

FEELINGS

4. Be an **understanding** person. Attitude is everything. Be open, flexible, generous and place yourself in the position of others. I am only interested in people's lives to learn or to help, not criticize.

5. **Self-control** and calmness is your condition. Activate it daily by doing physical and mental relaxation.

6. Get rid of **rage**. When you find yourself in this state, breathe and let the mind come down, so that you can act properly.

ACTIONS

7. Be **healthy**. Health is what you do every day. Eat a balanced diet, breathe fresh air and do breathing exercises. The more oxygen reaches all your body parts, the better. Do exercise and have your daily, weekly and annual rest. Do not forget to get close to nature, it is a source of health. Drink at least two liters of water and give up smoking and over drinking as soon as possible.

8. Take action. Problems are part of life. Make some of your best friends the questions: what, why, when and how.

9. It is all your **decision**. Use self-discipline, responsibility and persistence in the intelligent action.

10. Be **clear** in your mind about what you want, then do brainstorming. First, do not criticize, just think of options; second, study the most interesting options, plan, act, review and succeed.

"Before you criticize anyone, you should walk a thousand steps with his shoes."
Chinese proverb

EMOTIONAL

6.3 FROM UNCONSCIOUSNESS TO EMOTIONAL PROFICIENCY

Emotional intelligence is the ability to recognize your emotions, understand what they're telling you, and realize how your emotions affect people around you. Perception of others: when you understand how they feel, this allows you to manage relationships more effectively.

People with high emotional intelligence are usually **successful** in most things they do. Why? Because they're the ones that others want on their team. When they need help, they get it. Because they make others feel good, they go through life much more easily than people who are easily angered or upset. These are the skills:

1. **Self-Awareness**. Understand your emotions and do not let them rule over you. Take an honest look at yourself.

2. **Self-Regulation**. Characteristics are thoughtfulness, comfort with change, integrity and the ability to say no.

3. **Motivation**. Be willing to defer immediate pleasure for long-term success. Get used to challenges and learn effectiveness.

4. **Empathy**. This is the ability to identify with and understand the wants, needs and viewpoints of those around you.

5. **Social Skills**. It's usually easy to talk to and like people with good social skills. They can manage disputes, are excellent communicators and masters at building relationships.

6. Do a **self-evaluation**. What are your weaknesses? Are you willing to accept that you're not perfect and work on yourself?

7. Examine how you react to **stressful situations**.

8. Take **responsibility** for your actions.

9. Examine how your actions will **affect others**.

10. Observe how you **react** to people. Try to put yourself in their shoes, and be more open and accepting of their perspectives.

"**Bodily exercise, when compulsory, does no harm to the body; but knowledge which is acquired under compulsion obtains no hold on the mind.**"
Plato

6.4 FROM LACK OF CONTROL TO STABILITY OF CHARACTER

For most of us, our emotions seem to take over automatically, influencing how we think and how we behave, and consequently, how we conduct our lives. You can vastly increase your personal power by imposing more and more **conscious control** over your emotional states. Furthermore, your personal power tends to decrease to the extent that you indulge in negative emotions. I might also add that many of us habitually abdicate control to our negative emotions without ever realizing that doing so amounts to a tremendous waste of our lives.

1. **Brain physiology**. Learning how your brain works is an important aspect of emotional control. Once you realize that emotions are largely an automatic function of the human brain, it is much easier to learn how to begin controlling them.

2. Inappropriate **diet** and hormonal imbalances may affect your emotions adversely.

3. **Automatic thoughts**. In many instances our negative emotional responses are directly preceded by automatic thoughts. These automatic thoughts remain hidden for most people.

4. **Identification**. Emotional control is essentially a matter of detaching ourselves from our negative emotions.

5. **Freeze-framing** is a simple yet powerful technique for disengaging from negative emotions. You shift out of gear and into neutral. You freeze the thought and replace it with a positive one.

6. **Identify** the problematic areas (communication, eating, rage).

7. What positive thoughts and emotions can you **experience**?

8. Do **affirmations**: "I am relaxed, I am in control always!"

9. **Visualize** yourself being over any situation.

10. Discipline and **persistence** will help you become a more relaxed and understanding human being. Someone people will admire!

"**If you haven't forgiven yourself something, how can you forgive others.**"
Dolores Huerta, activist

PHYSICAL

6.5 FROM UNHEALTHY TO SPECTACULAR BODY

1. **Grace**. How many times does your loved one says I am sorry? And how many times do you forgive him or her? We all need grace at times, and so do you when it comes to taking care of your body. You do your exercises and diet for two entire weeks and then you might fall off the wagon. Analyze it, do not be too hard on yourself an go on.

2. **Daily attention**. To nurture a relationship you need to pay attention to what it needs. Your body needs adequate sleep, proper nutrition, exercise and plenty of water.

3. **Dream** a bit and get enthusiastic. What kind of body do you want to have? Maintain the image, work the plan and look great!

4. **Get excited** about your new looks. You will attract the opposite sex easily, feel great and be an example of self-control.

5. Be **flexible** but make determination of purpose your best friend. At first, it may be a bit hard, but you will see great results.

6. **Vitality** will be your new presentation card and cheerfulness your natural way of being. What else can you ask for?

7. Spend time and **listen**. In order to get to know someone you love, you need to spend time together. Your body is the same. It will only communicate with you if you listen. Someone I know says: "If you ignore your health, it will leave you."

8. **Special treats**. Sometimes you give your loved ones special treats to show you love them. Your body needs it, too. Treat yourself to a massage, a facial or new clothes every once in a while.

9. Have **fun**! Taking care of and loving your body doesn't have to be a drudgery. Adjust your attitude towards your body and your health. Find activities you love.

10. Get on a **plan** to reduce 10% fat with right attitude, proper nutrition, and sufficient water and rest.

"Cheerfulness and contentment are great beautifiers and are famous preservers of youthful looks."
Charles Dickens

6.6 FROM AN UNHEALTHY LIFESTYLE TO A HEALTHY LIFE

THOUGHTS

1. Keep a positive attitude and do **things** that make you happy. That is the best way to be happy and have a long healthy life.

2. Let your body tell you what it **needs**. It is quite clear. If you do not feel energetic and full of life, there is something wrong. Watch your diet, level of stress, exercise and your thoughts.

3. Always have something to feel **passionate** about, it could be your health, your wealth, your family and friends or your happiness.

FEELINGS

4. Stay **in touch** with family, friends and your community.

5. Remember to have these tools in your **suitcase**: humor, love, empathy, wisdom, motivation, self-control and strength.

6. Always be an **optimist**. Be a friend of love, affection, joy, laughing and hugging. They are the best antidote for physical problems and negative thoughts.

ACTIONS

7. Eat a balanced **diet**, including at least 5 fruits and vegetables a day, plenty of grains and fiber, lots of calcium-rich foods (dairy products, broccoli, tofu, canned sardines/salmon). Avoid caffeine and sugar.

8. Be physically **active** 30 minutes each day of activities like walking, dancing, yoga, gardening, playing golf, going for a long walk to keep both mind and body in good shape. Do not forget to sleep enough well.

9. Get regular preventive **checkups**. Be safe: always wear your seatbelt and bike helmet. Use smoke and carbon monoxide detectors in your homes. Keep your home well lit and free of things that could make you fall. Use medicine wisely. Follow directions and ask your doctor and pharmacists about side effects and drug interactions.

10. Keep your personal and **financial** records in order. Plan for your long-term housing and money needs.

"Plan for your long-term housing and money needs. Love is a great beautifier."
Louisa May Alcott, American novelist

SOCIAL

6.7 FROM BROKEN FAMILIES TO HAPPY FAMILIES

Dear friends, who has not been exposed to a certain degree of family conflicts in his/her life? Where two people live, conflict may arise. Conflict in any capacity can be a challenging path. Managing family conflict will take time and determination on many individual levels but can produce positive rewards over time through proper execution. Let me share with you some very important principles:

1. **Discuss** in detail the nature and full spectrum of the conflict. A clear understanding of the problem is crucial to the resolution.

2. Respond to the issues with "**mirrored listening**", which means the listener will repeat the stated comments back to the speaker to clearly display that he has been heard and understood accurately.

3. Create a **plan of action** that will clarify boundaries and expectations and will deal directly with resolving the conflict.

4. Move on and forget about hurt feelings or misunderstandings with others in your family. **Forgiveness** will heal the wounds that have occurred at a personal level.

5. Accept **compromise** in certain areas of your personal agenda. Relationships require give and take on many levels, and this compromise will bring resolutions and peace back into the home.

6. **Communicate**. Allow both parties to express what they are feeling and how they view the conflict situation.

7. Find Areas of **Agreement**. This helps initiate compromise and reduce the feeling that people are working against each other.

8. Try for a **Win-Win** Solution. It allows both parties to feel satisfied with the outcome of the conflict resolution.

9. Use a **Mediator**. That can be a healthy way to resolve conflict.

10. **Respect** Differences. You are as unique in your character and personality as the next person.

"You're searching, Joe, for things that don't exist; I mean beginnings. Ends and beginnings -- there are no such things. There are only middles."
Robert Frost

6.8 SOLVING COUPLE'S PROBLEMS

THOUGHTS

1. **Ask** yourself, "Is this person really available emotionally?' (People tend to spend more time researching a car purchase then their potential mate).

2. **Focus** on what you would like from your partner and what they have done right, instead of wrong.

3. Your **love** is returned. The person loves you back. You're not involved with somebody you're trying to get to love you.

FEELINGS

4. Be honest with yourself and ask: "Can I love this person exactly the way they are now without the expectation of change?" If not, you might have to consider finding the **right person** from the beginning.

5. Take responsibility for **expressing** your feelings and needs with one another. This will avoid conflict and deepen the emotional connection between you.

6. Continue **romancing** one another throughout the relationship, not just in the beginning stages. Have special nights!

ACTIONS

7. Take the time to create a genuine **emotional connection** and allow a passionate sexual relationship to grow.

8. Be **empathetic** to your partner. Put aside for the moment your need to be right and put yourself in your partner's shoes. Being understanding and validating your partner's feelings does not mean you have to agree with them in everything. Often feeling understood will mean more to your partner than being right or winning the battle.

9. Show **vulnerability**. Couples need to expose their authentic self. That entails being vulnerable and showing some emotional courage.

10. Be **yourself**. People are often afraid of revealing who they really are for fear that they will not be accepted.

"The best and most beautiful things in the world cannot be seen or even touched - they must be felt with the heart."
Helen Keller

PROFESSIONAL

6.9 FROM AN UNBALANCED LIFE TO WORK-FAMILY HARMONY

The most important thing I could say about balance: Preparation, intentionality and joint decision-making are the key to creating and maintaining the right family-work balance for you. Many couples experience extremely strong forces pulling them away from the priority that they would like their family to have. Without a clear plan and commitment to maintaining balance, time and energy for family erodes and evaporates. According to studies, successful couples used these strategies:

1. **Sharing housework** (negotiating equal division of labor).

2. Mutual, active involvement in **child care** (avoid monopolizing and controlling).

3. **Joint decision-making** (free expression of needs and negotiation). Reevaluating the meaning of success as a couple. Not only professional but also family matters.

4. Equal **financial** influence and previous commitment. Taking pride in the dual earning. Simple living, giving up some material amenities in order to reduce financial pressures.

5. **Valuing** both partners' work and life goals.

6. Sharing **emotional needs** (primacy of marital relationship, time alone and time with family and friends).

7. **Valuing family** as the highest priority over professional life.

8. Deriving enjoyment and purpose from **work**.

9. Actively setting **limits** on work by separating family and work (negotiation of working hours with employers).

10. Make a list of **essential activities** for the family. Learning to set priorities and limitations to other activities.

"Heaven never helps the man who will not act."
Sophocles

6.10 FROM BEING LOST TO HEALTHY AMBITION

One definition is an ardent desire for rank, fame or power. Also desire to achieve a particular end.

Ambition wakes you up in the morning. It motivates you to keep going when things get rough. But is ambition always a good thing? That's kind of like asking, "Is a knife a good thing?" The answer is the same: It all depends on how you use it. Let us look at healthy ambition.

1. There's a beautiful **vision**, in your head, of something you'd like to create, something you'd like to add to the world, or to your life experience.

2. You joyfully accept, or outright enjoy, the **steps** required to bring that vision to life.

3. You feel as good and whole during the **journey** toward your goal, as you imagine you will once you achieve it.

4. You still make time to cater for your **basic needs**, and the needs of those you are responsible for, as you work toward the goal.

5. To ensure that you're running on Healthy Ambition, remember that you are good **NOW**. You are whole NOW. Life is wonderful NOW.

6. There is nothing more that you need to BE in order to be happy NOW. There is nothing more that this moment requires in order to be perfect. Make the most out of every moment.

7. **Enjoy the journey.** Be present in every step toward the goal. Play with your kids. Take care of your health. Connect deeply and frequently with the people you love.

8. **Don't fast forward** past your life. Life is short enough... and you won't get to rewind.

9. From 1 to 10, are you enjoying the journey while striving toward an important goal? If you rate low, start **making changes**.

10. Know that unhealthy ambition affects other areas of your life with negative results (health, family, partner, friends).

"**You must learn to be still in the midst of activity and to be vibrantly alive in repose.**"
Indira Gandhi, Indian politician

7. HAVING
What do you want to have in your life?

GOD PLUTO

Do you want to have it all?

Start from the end, divide and achieve it all!

God of riches and good fortune

1. **How can you be more knowledgeable and positive?**

From lack of awareness and emotional poverty to practical knowledge and a rich emotional life

2. **How can you become the best you can be?**

From poor results and mediocrity to experience-based wisdom and the development of your full potential

3. **Do you want to have a wonderful family and fun?**

From family crisis and addictions to the construction of loving family bonds and healthy leisure time

4. **Do you want to be successful and an excellent professional?**

From failure and low performance to success and excellence

5. **How to find wealth and meaning in your life?**

From scarcity and emptiness to amazing wealth and life's purpose

7.1 FROM IGNORANCE TO YOUR POWERFUL MIND

I did a full-time degree in psychology and read many books on the marvelous power of the mind. One thing is for sure, science tells us that we still know very little about the full potential of the human mind. I can promise you one thing; the most powerful weapon in the world is above your shoulders. Use it well and you can have a phenomenal life.

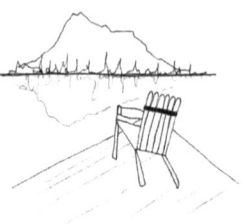

1. Realize that you are a **masterpiece**. From a very early age I was fascinated about human potential. I understood that people mainly are what they think of themselves, others and life.

2. You are what you think about most of the time. You want **achievements**? Do this: work on your motivation, have social support for weak moments, imagine success, your motto "Yes, I can," reward yourself physically and mentally and teach it.

3. **Program** you mind for your best! Increase pleasant and rewarding activities, do good planning, feel full of meaning and enthusiasm, keep a healthy balance between expectations and reality, live the present with love and share happiness everywhere.

4. You are the **creator** of your life. Bring to the present the best memories of the past, enjoy the present and hope for the best.

5. I feel part of the **Universe**. There is a universal energy that is everywhere and shapes all things. The stars and human beings have many chemical elements in common. We are star dust in reality.

6. It is a matter of **attitude**. Always look for the positive aspects, you will surely find them and be the shining star in the darkness.

7. Developing a **strong** personality. Make a very clear distinction between the events and your reaction to such events.

8. Use the **potential** of your mind, it is almost infinite.

9. Learn from **traumatic situations**. As they say: "If life gives you lemons, make lemonade." Learn and carry on!

10. **Be** the person and have the life you really want. See it, plan it and take action. Your affirmation: "From now on I only have positive and constructive thoughts, feelings and actions."

"Most folks are about as happy as they make up their minds to be."
Abraham Lincoln

7.2. FROM EMOTIONAL POVERTY TO RICHNESS

Positive emotions undo negative emotions and reduce the negative physical and psychological stresses of negative experiences. Negative emotions tell you that you are facing a win-loss encounter and need to take steps to engage with the obstacles. Positive emotions guide you to be more expansive, tolerant and creative so that you can maximize the social, intellectual and physical benefits of the situation.

Here are the top ten ways to generate more positive emotions.

1. **Increase** your happiness about the past by experiencing gratitude.

Gratitude amplifies savoring and appreciation of good events gone by.

2. Practice **forgiveness**. Adults who use an effective forgiveness tool have less anger, less stress, are more optimism and have better health.

3. Increase your happiness about the future by building **hope** and learning to be more optimistic.

You Were Born Happy!

4. Increase your happiness about the present by enjoying the healthy pleasures of the **moment**.

5. Experience **gratification**. This results from engagement in activities that exercise your natural strengths.

6. Use **appreciation**. Science confirms the wisdom of that advice.

7. Increase your **positive emotions** by identifying and nurturing your strengths. Break out of the weakness spiral and focus your attention on your natural talents and strengths and use them every day.

8. Focusing on your **strengths** is proving to be a more effective strategy than strengthening your weaknesses.

9. Increase your positive emotions by developing more of the "**Key Five**" strengths: gratitude, optimism, zest, curiosity and the ability to love and be loved.

10 Find yourself a **coach**, a counselor, a personal development consultant or a good self-help program and spend some time and resources in bringing more of the Key Five strengths into your life.

"**A woman must not depend upon the protection of man, but must be taught to protect herself.**"
Susan B. Anthony, women's activist

7.3 FROM POOR TO EXTRAORDINARY RESULTS

In 1923, at the Edgewater Beach Hotel in Chicago, eight of the world's wealthiest financiers met. These men controlled more money than the United States' government at that time. Twenty-five years later, some committed suicide, were insolvent or in prison.

Apparently they knew how to make money, but did not know much about life. Let us get acquainted with some facts about producing results in life:

1. **Money** is important and it will influence many of the decisions you make. Become prosperity conscious. Convince your imaginary subconscious that you are wealthy by vividly imagining the positive emotions your dream goals produce.

2. Be clear about **how much** you want and make a plan for it.

3. Image the **person** you should be to make that amount of money. Try to take action to develop those personality traits every day.

4. **Expect Abundance**. Program your "personal computer" to expect good results and that is exactly what you will receive.

5. Enjoy the **present**. It is the best way to attract positive results in the future.

6. Become a **mental magnet**. Everything you are seeking is seeking you in return. You will attract everything you focus on.

7. **Let Go and Let God**. There is a universal law. Just hold the image of your dreams in your mind and they will arrive.

8. Use the **law of vibration**. According to science, everything in this entire universe is connected. So, the way you attract is by creating a positive emotional expectancy of your dreams.

9. Be a **risk taker**. Please, forget the things that can go wrong, just focus on what you want to do and develop your abilities.

10. Be willing to **pay the price** of discipline for your dreams.

"Work joyfully and peacefully, knowing that right thoughts and right efforts will inevitably bring about right results."
James Allen

7.4 FROM MEDIOCRITY TO YOUR FULL POTENTIAL

While many of us are happy in life and do accomplish to some extent what we set out to do, there aren't many that actually push themselves that little bit further and go on to develop their full potential. While we might be particularly good at doing certain things in life, we could excel if only we had the courage and belief in ourselves to go for it.

THOUGHTS

1. Remember your youth. As children we are full of excellent ideas, they never stop flowing because we have an open mind and **belief** in ourselves that we can accomplish just about anything.

2. Remember that there is no right and wrong way of thinking, just focus on your skills and abilities and let your thoughts run free, put them to use and truly **excel** in life.

3. In order to be successful you should realize that you will sometimes make mistakes, no one is perfect and mistakes are ok providing you acknowledge them and **learn** from them.

FEELINGS

4. Having **patience**. Things don't happen overnight, so have patience and you will be rewarded.

5. **Determination**. Stick to your guns and never give in when things don't go your way or you come across hurdles.

6. **Commitment**. Be committed towards your goals and what you want to achieve, set goals in mind and don't let anything stand in the way.

ACTIONS

7. **Working hard**. Put everything you have got into everything you do when working towards what you want in life.

8. **Organizational skills**. The more organized you are, the easier the road to success will be. Plan out your ideas to their fullest.

9. Learn from **mistakes**. You will make mistakes along the way but you can learn valuable lessons from these and move on.

10. **Confidence** in yourself. You have to be self-confident and believe in yourself and your ideas, there is no room for doubt.

"**We are all pencils in the hand of God writing love letters to the world.**"
Mother Theresa, social worker

7.5 FROM LIMITATION TO ABUNDANCE AWARENESS

This is the story of a minister and a farmer. Many years ago, a minister was driving along a remote country road, when suddenly he saw a very beautiful farm. A farmer was working the field. As the farmer got closer the minister smiled, raised his arm, and waved saying: "My good man, God has certainly blessed you with a beautiful farm!"  The farmer stopped, wiped the sweat from his sun-scorched brow and with a slow voice said:"Yes Reverend, you're right." God has blessed me with a beautiful farm, but I just wish you could have seen it when he had all to himself!"

Now, become aware you can be the writer, producer and director of the constant movie you have in your mind. Everything we do is preceded by an **image**. We think first in order to form an image, then we do the work. Therefore, I would like to encourage you to want to have it all: a powerful mind, a rich emotional life, the ability to produce the results you want, the pride of an extraordinary personality, the best you can be in your personal relationships, the success you deserve, excellence in your profession, the capacity to have several sources of income, a life of purpose and the potential to be happier, healthier and wealthier.

The way to do it is by becoming the person you want to **be** first. Develop your ability to love, to share, to forgive, to help others do the same with their lives. Always find the time to work on your mind, feeling and body first, then dedicate time to your loved ones, your friends and the community. If you think it is right for you and brings you benefit, develop your spiritual side and try to leave the people you meet and the world a bit better than you found it.

"Ever tried. Ever failed. No matter. Try Again. Fail again. Fail better."
Samuel Beckett

7.6 FROM ADDICTIONS TO HEALTHY LEISURE TIME

Taking time for leisure activities, apart from the demands of work and other responsibilities, helps people function better physically and mentally. In fact, the more time spent doing different types of enjoyable activities, the better a person's health tends to be, according to scientific studies.

"People who are engaged in multiple enjoyable activities are better off physically and psychologically," said study co-author **Karen A. Matthews**, Ph.D. She is a professor of psychiatry, epidemiology and psychology at the University of Pittsburgh School of Medicine in the United States of America.

THOUGHTS

1. Keep in mind the positive effects of doing some kind of **sport**.

2. Be open to the world of **arts** (music, dance, theatre, opera, ballet, painting, sculpture, cinema and all social cultural expressions).

3. Make the habit of enjoying a **lifestyle** with leisure time activities that promote not only the health of your family members but also of the community as a whole.

FEELINGS

4. Be **enthusiastic** about improved health and teach your kids to follow the example. Sport activities help them make friends, succeed at school and become more active, and improves their self-image.

5. Leisure activities restores the mind-body **harmony**.

6. Other social activities can create **special moments** with loved ones.

ACTIONS

7. The more people engaged in physical activity during their spare time, the less likely they were to be **depressed**.

8. Identify two **resources** that can be used to locate healthy leisure time activities (e.g., newspaper, Internet, bulletin board, phone book, family and friends).

9. Identify various leisure time activities for further **exploration**.

10. Organize **regular events** where several people are involved.

"The future belongs to those who believe in the beauty of their dreams."
Eleanor Roosevelt, activist

7.7 FROM FAILURE TO SUCCESS

I have always been fascinated about success since I was very young. It wasn't until I became a LifeSuccess consultant with Bob Proctor in 2011 that I realized the far-reaching consequences and the importance of success in our lives.

Let me give you some suggestions to achieve real success:

Let us start with the **mind**. **First**, the starting point for achievement is a strong desire, not a hope, not a wish, but a burning desire, which transcends everything else. It must be definite. **Second**, use the incredible power behind auto-suggestion. You repeat affirmations to yourself every day with a lot of emotion, take the necessary actions and let go, results will start taking place in your life. **Third**, use your imagination. Einstein said that imagination is much more powerful than knowledge, and great minds mention that what you can conceive, you can achieve.

In the **emotional** world, you can focus on three very powerful concepts. **First**, believe in yourself and in your incredible power. If you don't, no one else will. **Second**, Get rid of fear. Protect yourself from negative influences, whether of your own making, or the result of the activities of negative people around you. **Third**, recognize that you have the mental ability of will-power. Put it to constant use until you build a mental wall of immunity.

Action, action and action! This is the most crucial aspect that separates achievers from non-achievers. **First**, persistence will take you wherever you want to go, only if you persist enough. **Second**, learn to harness the power of decisions. **Third**, the more specialized knowledge you have, the greater the demand for your service. **Finally**, start a Master Mind group, a group of like-minded individuals who support each other to become more successful.

Action may not always bring happiness; but there is no happiness without action."
Benjamin Disraeli

7.8 FROM LOW PERFORMANCE TO EXCELLENCE

Today's organizations place great emphasis on personal responsibility and initiative. Managing yourself effectively and working productively with others is critical to both your professional success and the success of your organization.

Let us see key characteristics of professional people. The main components of personal effectiveness are:

1. **Realize** your strengths and fulfill your potential. Evaluate your aptitudes, styles and potential growth areas. You can always do a personal strengths inventory and work from there.

2. Building your professional **reputation**. Be relaxed, slow but steady and help all those around you become better.

3. Enhance your **thinking** tool set. Understand thinking (limiting beliefs) and human interaction processes.

3. One the most sought-after abilities in the working world is the capacity to produce **excellent results** under pressure. Become good.

4. Identify important **players** in your environment, be able to work with difficult coworkers and be assertive.

5. Build productive **relationships** with upper management, try to always do a bit more than you are supposed to. This technique alone will speed up your professional progression.

6. Understand how to manage **stress** effectively. Be calm in the mind, relax your body and control your emotions.

7. Amplify your effectiveness by **networking**.

8. Develop your ability to **talk in public**, both in theory and praxis.

9. Design a personal success strategy, identify short and long-term goals and achieve balance with the **Wheel of Life**.

10. Control your **work environment**, tidy office and desk, handle interruptions, handle e-mail domination and plan your day.

"Love often leads to healing, while fear and isolation breed illness. And our biggest fear is abandonment."
Candace Pert, neuroscientist

7.9 FROM SCARCITY TO AMAZING WEALTH

Multiple Sources of Income (MSI)

Bob Proctor is one of the most sought-after speakers in the world for professional coaching and company seminars and a Teacher in the wildly popular film, *The Secret*. Mr. Proctor is considered one of the living masters and teachers of the Law of Attraction. For over 50 years, Bob Proctor has focused his work and teachings on helping people use the power of their mind to achieve prosperity, rewarding relationships and spiritual awareness. He is the best-selling author of "*You Were Born Rich*" and has transformed the lives of millions through his books, seminars, courses and personal coaching. He taught me this technique, **MSI**.

What is it? This is a technique that will permit you to multiply your present income by providing service beyond that which you are presently providing at your primary source of income (your work). **Additional Service-Additional Income**. It will earn many times what you are earning now. It is based on the law of compensation: the more service you give, the more income you get.

What is it not? This is not a part-time activity. The idea is to create the structure to get passive income, without working for it.

What can you do? You can add ideas to this list constantly.

1. Write a book, son, play, movie script or any other.

2. Create your own web site where people can buy from you.

3. Join a network marketing company.

4. Produce a series of CDs/DVDs in your chosen field of expertise.

5. Invent something. The more useful, the higher the impact.

6. Invest in real estate and watch it grow.

7. Refer clients or market something to others and get a fee for it.

8. Web based affiliate programs.

9. Franchise something.

10. Rent you mailing list for a fee.

Start seeing opportunities everywhere to provide a good service!

"You can have it all."
Bob Proctor

7.10 FROM EMPTINESS TO LIFE'S PURPOSE

Dear reader, I believe life is a gift. There are so many choices to make in life and our direction for career, family, friends and recreation can change at the drop of a hat. When we have a sense of purpose and direction, then we can be productive and fulfilled. I would like to share with you some principles I live by:

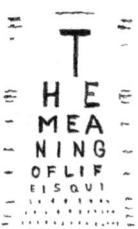

1. Live a **purpose-driven life** by determining your focus statement. Take time to think about what you want your life to say about you.

2. Understand that nothing in life happens by accident. Motivation guides us, as we live a purpose-driven life. Some are motivated by negative emotions such as anger, fear, guilt or the need to acquire more things. Some are motivated by the need to please other people all the time. Decide what is important to you. Choose to be motivated by hope, courage, love and the knowledge that you are not an accident. You were created to **contribute** something good to society.

3. Know that living on purpose is not so much about jobs, hobbies or places you visit in your spare time. Make a decision to not just be pulled in to the status quo in the culture around you, but to focus your life on a higher purpose like living in **love, joy and peace**.

4. Remember that after we're gone, it's not the stuff we leave behind that will matter for eternity. It will be what kind of character we had and the **example** we lived for others that will matter.

5. **Discover** your purpose. Ask yourself, let it come out, don't judge.

6. **Plan** to integrate it into your daily activities. Make changes.

7. **How do I know?** Do you feel passionate about it? Yes? Perfect!

8. **Analyze it.** Do not let your present cultural or social context interfere with what you really feel inside. If there is conflict, you will have to either change the purpose or the context.

9. Transform purpose into **specific goals** and follow the plan.

10. **Be proud**, not many people can say they have a purpose!

"As long as you believe what you're doing is meaningful, you can cut through fear and exhaustion and take the next step."
Arlene Blum

8. PROFESSION
How do you find a professional activity that makes you rich and passionate?

GOD MERCURY

God`s gift to you is more talent and ability than you can possibly image,

Your gift to God is to use such talent and ability as much as you can for the service of others

God of trade, profit and commerce

1. **What is your dream profession?**

From frustration and routine to your dream profession and realization

2. **Do you want to have a clear career plan?**

From lack of planning and the burn-out feeling to a career plan and constant development

3. **Do you want to master the art of human relations and stress control?**

From professional failures and stress to human relations expert and well-being

4. **What is your gift to your loved ones and the world?**

From social inexistence and inferiority to social influence and your unique gift to the world

5. **How to find your dream profession?**

From low pay and meaningless activity to high income and personal fulfillment

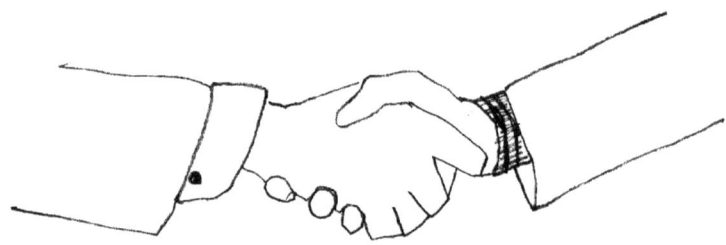

8.1 FROM FRUSTRATION TO YOUR DREAM PROFESSION

Barbara Brown was the first to make the public aware of scientists' findings in relation to career plan. **First**, put everything you know about yourself on a piece of paper. Knowing yourself is the best way to making the right decisions. **Second**, use some kind of graphic to organize the information. **Finally**, put every-  thing in order of importance. As **Richard Nelson** mentions in his international bestseller "*What Color is Your Parachute?*" this graphic could look like a flower. Let us have a look at the petals:

1. **My favorite interests.** What fascinates you the most? Do a systematic inventory of the transferable skills (you can employ in different job positions) that you already possess. Then name jobs that fit with it. The yellow pages and Internet can help!

2. **Geography**: places in order of priority. You can start by doing research on the local organizations that interest you. Find out what problems they have and how they try to solve them.

3. **My favorite people environments.** Once you know, what you want, go out and talk to people who are doing it. I am sure they will tell you all about it. Find out all you can and be thankful. When you are ready, seek out the person who actually has the power to hire you where you want.

4. **My favorite values and goals.** What skills do you most enjoy using? These are the transferable skills you can use anywhere. Remember, the higher the skills, the less competition you face!

5. **My favorite working conditions.** What kind of data, people or things do you enjoy working with? You can think of previous work you didn't like and start seeking the opposite.

6. **Salary and level of responsibility.** Start with a minimum to cover your monthly expenses and "get by." Maximum could be astronomical. So, be realistic, with your present competency and experience. Think also of your possible progression.

"Never leave that till tomorrow which you can do today."
Benjamin Franklin

8.2 FROM ROUTINE TO HAPPINESS AT WORK

THOUGHTS

1. **Choose** to Be Happy at Work. As in life, happiness is an option you decide to take.

2. **Commitments** You Can Keep. Just walk your talk!

3. Take Charge of Your Own Professional and **Personal Development**. You are the person with the most to gain from continuing to develop professionally. Take charge of your own growth.

FEELINGS

4. Do Something You **Love** Every Single Day. You may or may not love your current job and you may or may not believe that you can find something in your current job to love, but you can. Trust me.

5. **Avoid Negativity**. Choosing to be happy at work means avoiding negative conversations, gossip and unhappy people.

6. Practice **Professional Courage**. If you are like most people, you don't like conflict. And the reason why is simple. You've never been trained to participate in meaningful conflict, so you likely think of conflict as scary, harmful and hurtful. Conflict can be all three. However, done well, conflict can also help you

accomplish your work mission and your personal vision. Conflict can help you serve customers and create successful products.

ACTIONS

7. Take **Responsibility** for knowing what is happening at work. Seek out the information you need to work effectively. Develop an information network and use it.

8. Ask for **feedback** frequently. Ask your boss for feedback. Tell him you'd really like to hear his assessment of your work.

9. Make **friends**. Liking and enjoying your coworkers are hallmarks of a positive, happy work experience. Take time to get to know them. You might actually like and enjoy them.

10. If all else fails, start working on your **plan to leave** the job and work for yourself or change professions/jobs.

"When will our consciences grow so tender that we will act to prevent human misery rather than avenge it?"
Eleanor Roosevelt, activist

8.3 FROM LACK OF PLANNING TO A JOB HUNT PLAN

I don't know how many jobs I have done in my life. Imagine, twenty years in several countries. Let me share with you some things I learned about finding work along the way:

1. How do employers look for new employees? You should **adapt** your strategy to theirs. From within, you can always start at the bottom or as part-time. Using proof, show them what you can do. Using a best friend or a business colleague. Using an agency they trust. Using an ad they have placed.

2. **What do you want?** It is vital to know what characteristics your dream profession should have (salary, location, activity).

3. **Employer's mind.** Why are you here, what can you do for us, what kind of person are you? What distinguishes you from other people who can do the same as you, and can I afford you?

163

4. **How to deal with handicaps**. If you have a handicap or think you have one, it cannot possibly prevent you from getting hired. It can only prevent you from getting hired at some places.

5. **Interviews**: The employer's fears. An interview is like dating, it is two people trying to decide to go steady. Be part of the solution, not the problem and show evidence.

6. **How much help is Internet?** Take advantage of the benefits but it will not get you a job. You do that with real contact.

7. **The best way to hunt for a job**. First, doing a life-changing job-hunt. You must do extensive homework on yourself before you start looking. Second, create a job club, use the phone book to identify fields of interest and ask for a position you do well. Third, knock on the door of employers that interest you. Finally, ask for job-leads to family, friends, career centers.

8. **Matching** your personality with your dream job.

9. Use your **contacts**; they can connect you with a job.

10. **Resumes**: be as attractive as possible without lies.

**"I know nothing except the fact of my ignorance."
Socrates**

8.4 FROM THE BURNT-OUT FEELING TO CONSTANT DEVELOPMENT

Michael Jeffrey Jordan (born February 17, 1963) is a former American professional basketball player, active businessman, and majority owner of the Charlotte Bobcats. He has been considered to be the greatest basketball player of all time. But it wasn't always like that. During his sophomore year he tried out for the varsity team but was considered to be too short (5'11'-1,80 m). Motivated to prove his worth, he became the star of his team and there starts the legend. He can teach us many lessons:

THOUGHTS

1. There are **opportunities everywhere**. The intelligent person knows how to recognize them and make the most out them when they arrive.

2. A great **success formula** is patience, persistence, self-discipline.

3. Be aware that you will be as successful as the human level of those you surround yourself with.

FEELINGS

4. Be **open to others**. Remember that there are more honest and good people in the world than the opposite.

5. Let **love** be your guide. Show confidence in people and they will respond doing more for you. Your reward will be a greater number of opportunities, luck and success.

6. Real affective wealth is to love and **respect** life and everything in it. It is loving yourself, the world and humanity.

ACTIONS

7. Show **compassion** for others. Say no to hate, resentment and jealousy, as they will bring misery to your life.

8. **Share** your wealth, creating opportunities that others can benefit from. Don't give them fish, show them how to fish!

9. There are **universal laws**. Integrate your spiritual and financial areas and your life will benefit in all aspects.

10. Create your **own business**. There is no wealth limit and have always several plans, in case one or two of them do not work out.

"**There is Michael Jordan and then there is the rest of us.**"
Magic Johnson

8.5 FROM DIFFICULTIES TO NEGOTIATION EXPERT

I remember once in my early twenties having a conversation with a friend about a new job he was about to start. He was quite excited about such an achievement but when I asked him about the salary he looked at me quite surprised and said: "The money is not that important." Well, I guess it was important because he was quite depressed when he learned how much they were going to pay him! Please, let us be honest. The salary is important. Probably not the most important thing but surely one of the main criteria for choosing a job or profession. The problem is that we find it very difficult to negotiate our worth. Let me share with you some suggestions:

1. Never discuss salary **until the end** of the interviewing process, when they have definitely said they want you.

2. The purpose of salary negotiation is to uncover **the most** that an employer is willing to pay to get you.

3. During the salary discussion, try **never to be the first one** to mention a salary figure.

4. **Never lose heart**. Let statistics be on your side. The rule of thumb in sales is that if you want to make a sale, you should contact at least ten potential clients.

5. **Separate** people from issues and build a good relationship.

6. **Win-win** situations. Always come up with new and creative ideas that are beneficial for both parties in any area of life.

7. Before you go to the interview, do some research on typical **salaries** for your field and organization (Internet, people). Do not forget social benefits (health insurance, vacation, travel).

8. Define a **salary range** and the minimum you would accept.

9. Learn how to **close** the deal. Ask for written contract.

10. Preparation of **several plans** is always an intelligent option. Have several alternatives for what you can do next, for approaching your job-hunt, for job prospects, for "target" organizations and for approaching your next potential employer.

"**The basic test of freedom is perhaps less in what we are free to do than in what we are free not to do.**"
Eric Hoffer

8.6 FROM EMPLOYEE TO BUSINESSMAN

J K Rowling was born in Yate, Gloucestershire, England. She attended school and found her love for writing fantasy stories. She would often write stories and tell them to her sister. Rowling moved from village to village many times and often traveled. In December of 1990, Rowling's mother died, and she moved to Porto, Portugal, in order to teach English as a foreign language. Before her mother's death, Rowling had already begun writing her famous Harry Potter novel. In Portugal, Rowling married, but the couple separated in 1993. However, she did have a daughter and the two moved to Edinburgh, Scotland. During this time, Rowling was diagnosed with clinical depression and often contemplated suicide. She was unemployed and living on welfare. She was able to write and complete her first novel by going to several different cafés. Today, J.K. Rowling is worth about **$1.1 billion** and has been able to sell over **400 million books**.

There are **many options** before setting up your business. You can stay where you live now or move to a new place. You can continue in your present career or start a new one. You can do temporary work or follow the same career in a new place. Go back to school for retraining or work and study at the same time. You can work for yourself and work from home. Whatever you do, I suggest you have some "security" earnings in case things do not work out as planned and have the mental attitude to do whatever it takes to face any situation.

It takes a lot of guts to try anything in today's economy. Please, keep these rules in mind. **First**, you can take risks but make them manageable. **Second**, talk to other people who have done the same or something similar. **Third**, have a plan B before you start. Besides, if you are sharing your life with someone else, discuss it thoroughly. **Next**, better to move gradually to self-employment while keeping your regular job. **Finally**, you only have one life and it is yours to do what you feel it is right for you. All the best in whatever you decide!

"It was we, the people; not we, the white male citizens; but we, the whole people, who formed the Union."
Susan B. Anthony, feminist

8.7 FROM UNPREPAREDNESS TO WAR TACTICS

The 33 Strategies of War by **Robert Greene** is a "guide to the subtle social game of everyday life inspired by the military principles in war." It is composed of discussions and examples on offensive and defensive strategies from a wide variety of people and conditions.

The book is divided into five parts. This a very condensed summary and I adapted the vocabulary to everyday social situations. I hope it is useful for various life challenges:

1. **Self-Directed Warfare**. The good strategist must take three steps. First, be aware of your weaknesses. Second, make the continuous improvement philosophy your best travel companion. Third, keep your mental focus on the positive side of things.

2. **Organizational (Team) Warfare**. We can all be brilliant individually but the real achievements are carried out by teams. First, have only one authority at the top level and avoid leadership confusion. Second, give your team members clear indications of the goals. Finally, always keep a high level of motivation.

3. **Defensive Warfare.** As they say: "the best offense is a good defense." The prerequisites are simple. First, make the most out of your own resources, focusing your energies only on those matters that are worthy of you. Second, a retreat can also mean victory. Learn what went wrong and apply it next time. Finally, when you are fully prepared, take massive action to achieve your goal.

4. **Offensive Warfare.** Be prepared for unexpected events. Best thing is to take the initiative and create your own circumstances. Plan, take action, review your progress and reward yourself.

5. **Unconventional (Dirty) Warfare.** Unfortunately nowadays it seems as though the moral right way of doing things is gone. Therefore, be aware of it, but I suggest the reader to be an example of good and positive values and principles. That will make you happier than the opposite option.

"The first and most important step toward success is the feeling that we can succeed."
Nelson Boswell

8.8 FROM INDIVIDUALITY TO TEAM WORK

No matter what you call your team-based improvement effort: continuous improvement, total quality, lean manufacturing or self-directed work teams, you are striving to improve results for **customers**. Few organizations, however, are totally pleased with the results their team improvement efforts produce. If your team improvement efforts are not living up to your  expectations, this self-diagnosing checklist may tell you why. Successful team building, that creates effective, focused work teams, requires attention to each of the following principles:

1. You are too small to do everything by yourself. The more **interaction among members** the better it will work.

2. **The goal** is more important than individual participation and the leader makes the difference between two similar teams.

3. Every team member has a place of excellence and such excellent performance must be promoted through **training**.

4. As **challenges** grow, the need for team work also grows. The greater the team, the greater will be its impact on the image of the leader.

5. Any team is as strong as its weakest member. **Leaders** should realize this fact and solve it as soon as possible.

6. Successful teams have members who make things happen. It is crucial to have a couple of members who **inspire** the rest of the team.

7. Create an environment of mutual **trust**, great collective force and shared values. The vision of the team must be clear at all times.

8. Bad attitude is contagious. However, nothing hurts when the team is **winning**. Take care of negative aspects and promote success and high levels of individual and team motivation.

9. **The price** of hard work and discipline must be paid. Leaders should be living examples of positive qualities members can emulate.

10. **Redefine goals** as you go along, as situations do change.

"Only the dreamer shall understand realities, though in truth his dreaming must be not out of proportion to his waking."
Chinese Proverb

8.9 FROM LOW PAY TO A MILLION DOLLARS!

Do you want to make a million dollars a year?

Use the Wheel of Fortune

This Wheel is the accumulation of the different sources you want your income to come from. You decide how many you want. Give yourself time everyday to dream, to think of the multiple ways in which you could generate income even when you sleep.

There are three money earning strategies to consider:

1. **Trading time for money.** This is done by 96% of the population. By the way, a job means "Just over broke."

2. **Investing money**, 3% of the population.

3. **Multiple sources.** Only 1%.

You should have the amount you need to provide for all the things you want in your life and lead a happy life with your loved ones and friends. You can have it all. The only limit to your earning capacity is the **limit you place on yourself**.

This is just one idea. You can come up with your own. **Think and grow rich**. You have a jewel of unlimited potential above your shoulders. Let your imagination run wild and then take action until you achieve your dream. You will not regret it! Let me give you just a couple of options. Do you want to make one million dollars a year? You know, it can be a lot or it could be little. That all depends on your interpretation. Divide and win:

1. If you work 250 days x $4,000 daily = $ 1,000,000 yearly

2. If you work 200 days x $5,000 daily = $ 1,000,000 yearly

3. If you work 100 days x $10,000 daily = $ 1,000,000 yearly

"I know the plans I have for you, declares the Lord, plans to prosper you and not to harm you, plans to give you hope and a future."

(Jeremiah 29:11)

8.10 FROM EMPLOYEE TO MILLIONAIRE

Employees do become Millionaires! There are thousands of "Average Joe's" and "Average Jane's" working right next to you who have a **million dollars** in their bank and their investments. You can do the same if you just follow the secrets that all of them used.
Those secrets are simple, clear and available to everyone who wants to apply them to life:

1. Keep your eyes open for **better ways** to do your job.

2. Don't be afraid to **negotiate**. According to studies, you will boost your pay by 7.4%.

3. **Quantify** how much your efforts add to the company's bottom line. If that's not feasible, spotlight your value with comparable salaries for workers in your position from a Web site, such as **Salary.com**.

4. Plot your strategy when it's time to move on. Create a professional-looking **page** on social media.

5. **Milk your benefits**. Contribute as much as you can to your 401(k) and other tax-deferred retirement plans.

6. Flex your **tax-saving muscle**. Learn how to pay taxes intelligently.

7. **Invest** like crazy. Don't delay. The quicker you get a jump on putting money aside, the easier it will be to stuff a seven-figure cushion.

8. **Invest automatically**, either through your employer's retirement plan or by setting up a regular deposit to a mutual fund or broker.

9. Watch for **fund fees**. The more you pay, the tougher it is to earn an above-average return.

10. **Keep it simple**. Be wary of get-rich-quick schemes.

9. FINANCES

How can you gain financial independence to enjoy life to the fullest?

GODDESS ABUNDIA

Find your life´s purpose and the money will follow.

Earn, spend and invest the difference.

Goddess of success, prosperity, abundance, good fortune and protector of savings, investments and wealth

1. **Do you want to find the unstoppable force that will lead you to riches?**

From indetermination and insecurity to the force of clarity and determination

2. **The plan.**

From uncertainty to your road map and results

3. **Strategies to accelerate and protect your wealth.**

From fear to ambition and dreams

4. **Your tool bag.**

From weakness into strength and power

5. **Integration: mastering your future.**

From despair to hope and achievement

9.1 FROM INDETERMINATION TO THE UNSTOPPABLE FORCE OF CLARITY

THINK LIKE A MILLIONAIRE

I am not a millionaire yet but I am following the principles millionaires have used and I am producing great results. Let me share them with you:

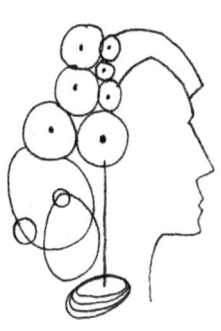

Let us start with your **mind**. **First**, where do you start? Believe that you will achieve your dreams, your situation will not change unless you do something, have a passionate desire to improve your life, dare to dream big and eliminate negative thoughts. **Second**, wealth is a mental state. Create your own affirmations and use them every day, repeat positive words to yourself frequently, make a list of talents you want to develop, do it and repeat it to yourself. **Finally**, help your environment become wealthier and your environment will make you wealthier (contacts, projects, clients, sales, income, benefits, financing).

Work on your emotions. Do what you like, that is the most powerful emotional motivation. Think about your life. How is it? How do you want it to be? Ask yourself: "If I had all the money and time, and could not fail, what would I do?" Go to sleep asking your subconscious or the universal mind or God how you can be wealthier and act upon the answers!

Be the best you can be in your present position and learn how to create your own company. Save money, gain as much experience as you can, use your free time to work on your future company, keep raising your intellectual capacity with training and make as many professional contacts as you can. Start your own company as you continue working on your current position.

"**Dream, believe and take massive action!**"
Oscar Escallada

9.2 FROM INSECURITY TO POWER

THE IMPOSSIBLE IS POSSIBLE

THOUGHTS

1. Easy ways are worthless. What is the difference between an obstacle and an opportunity? Our **attitude**. As Luo Holtz said: "Show me someone who has done something extraordinary, and I will show you someone who conquered adversity."

2. **Impossible?** You decide. As the Bible mentions: "When you get close to God, God gets close to you."

3. **The search is what counts!** Are you just trembling about an uncertain future or are you going towards the realization of your dreams with firm step and a smile on your face? There are many ideas around you that are worth a million dollars!

FEELINGS

4. **Feel the fear and do it anyway!** You must get on the football field if you want to score a goal!. If you worry too much about the future, soon there will be no future to worry about.

5. **Passion is all you need.** You have the ability to develop as much passion in your life as you want, why don't you do it? Your life will be transformed in a matter of seconds.

6. **Control your emotions.** If you lose your head, how do you plan to use it? The best way you can use your time is by getting on with the projects you set for yourself, not fixing the actions of bad temper.

ACTIONS

7. **Get up one more time than you fall.** Have you ever failed at something? Welcome to the club! And what do we do now? Just learn from the experience and don't you dare to give up until you succeed.

8. Your best friends make you be your best. In what direction do you want to go? Take a look at the **people** who surround you.

9. The key to success is your **daily routine**. Have a look at the seeds of what you are planting every day and that will be what you reap.

10. **Miracles** start in your heart. When you look at the world with an open and friendly heart, what kind of world do you see?

"**No life ever grows great until it is focused, dedicated and disciplined.**"
Author Unknown

9.3 FROM THE LABYRINTH OF CONFUSION TO FOCUS AND ACTION PLAN

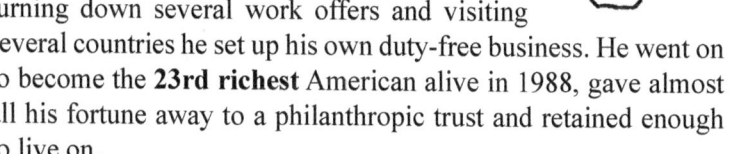

Charles Feeney was born into an Irish-American family in blue-collar New Jersey in 1931. The family was lucky enough to make ends meet even through the Great Depression. He was bright and had a talent for making money from odd jobs. Charles graduated in hotel management and paid his way by selling sandwiches around campus at night. After turning down several work offers and visiting several countries he set up his own duty-free business. He went on to become the **23rd richest** American alive in 1988, gave almost all his fortune away to a philanthropic trust and retained enough to live on.

Keep your **mind focused** on your dreams. First, be aware that broken focus is the number one reason so many projects go uncompleted, so many commitments go unfulfilled and so many dreams go unattained. Second, you must be in the right state of mind. A lack of focus can be brought on by negative feelings, intrusive thoughts, negative talk from your inner chatterbox. Third, eliminate all distractions. The first rule of focus is this: "Wherever you are, be there." Next, set time parameters for every task. Don't just spend your time without achieving what you want. Rest when you must, but stick to your plan! Finally, do one thing at a time.

"Often he who does too much does too little."
Italian Proverb

Focus → Power → Action → Progress

An **action plan** is vital to know where you are going. You can apply the same principles to your life than those of a business plan. Set concrete goals, responsibilities and deadlines to guide your business. Plan tasks to people or departments and set milestones and deadlines for tracking implementation. Finally, as part of the implementation, it should provide regular review and course corrections.

"Success usually comes to those who are too busy to be looking for it."
Henry David Thoreau (1817-1862)

9.4 PERSONAL ABILITIES — THE METAMORPHOSIS

THOUGHTS

1. Why is **financial intelligence** important? Anybody would say that they need more money but the important thing in my view is to know why, mainly because trying to increase your income may affect your present life balance. I think the most important thing is that money gives you freedom. **Freedom** to be the person you want to be, freedom to do the things you want to do when you want or need and freedom to be with the people you love.

2. Differentiate between **knowing and selling**. In the United States, the richest country in the world, less than 5 % of the population earn more than 100,000 dollars a year. Thousands of brilliant people with doctor's degrees are having financial problems. The great ability they are lacking is selling. Your goal? Become a expert in sales.

3. Keep the **balance**. One lesson life taught me: the shortest way to happiness is balance in life's areas. Try to improve your health, your professional performance, your bank account, but don't lose balance.

FEELINGS

4. Develop **abundance** consciousness. Many experts say that you attract what you are. So, fill your mind with positive expectancy.

5. Put your **heart** in your actions. That alone will make you happy.

6. Do what you **love** and the money will follow. It is not a luxury but a necessity if you want to lead a really prosperous life.

ACTIONS

7. **Produce** more money. Find solutions to problems.

8. **Protect** your wealth. Know the rules of the game.

9. Have a **budget**. Income − Outcome = save the difference.

10. **Leverage** your money. Study your investment options.

"Whatever you think having money will give you – aliveness, peace, self-esteem – is the quality you need to develop to become more magnetic to money and abundance. View money and things not as something you create to fill a lack, but as tools to help you more fully express yourself and realize your potential."
Author unknown

9.5 FROM LIMITS TO WORLD VIEW

THE SECRETS OF RICH PEOPLE

My intention in the following section is not to make you feel miserable by comparison with the richest people on earth but to summarize some of the principles they used and let you know that some of them were once absolutely normal or even poor and went through real hardship. Here they are:

What is a multimillionaire? Someone who has more than 1,000 million dollars. How many are there? According to Forbes magazine, the number of multimillionaires is 797. The United States and Canada have 395, Germany 55, Europe and Asia 210, South East Asia and Australia 115, Middle East and Africa 53 and Latin America 24. What can they teach us? Some of them have built their lives around the following principles:

1. The desire to make beautiful things and leave a **legacy**. The desire to provide value for money and a **great service**.

2. The properties and wealth they could leave their **children**. Every parent wants to care for their children when they are gone.

3. **Patronage** to noble causes. Several reasons have been given: be forgiven for their wealth, personal gratification, narcissism, fiscal, political or social benefits.

4. **Change the world** in some way, create a new society, invent something new, achieve great successes.

5. The human spirit of inconformity and **self-improvement**. Where would the human race be if past generations had been perfectly comfortable with their situations and conditions?

6. Create great **masterpieces** in the arts.

7. The **passion** to improve personal conditions.

8. The men and women who could not settle for less than they **could be**.

9. Being in "**the game**," losing, winning and having fun.

10. Intelligence, drive and desire for a **better future** for all.

"**Our loyalties must transcend our race, our tribe, our class, and our nation; and this means we must develop a world perspective.**"
Martin Luther King

9.6 FROM REALITY TO REALIZATION OF YOUR DREAMS

BALANCE OF WEALTH & WEALTH OF BALANCE

This play on words just came to my mind. On the one hand, in order to create wealth, you need balance. You need to have a clear mind, feel positive and passionate and take massive action. On the other hand, real wealth is balance. A balanced life of intellectual, emotional, professional and spiritual areas.

Here you have an example of a "**Balanced Life Wheel.**" Score yourself (with ten being the highest level of achievement), then shade in from the center out. This will show how balanced your life is... or how much out of balance it is. With a different color or pattern, shade in where you would like to be in six month's time. Then make a plan of how you will work towards achieving these goals.

1. **Thinking**: Learning, reading, training and having a clearly defined life purpose and working towards fulfilling it.

2. **Feeling**: Be in touch with and express feelings creatively.

3. **Actions**: Define and follow your life's plan.

4. **Individual being**: What personality traits or virtues do you want?

5. **Social being**: Close, intimate and nurturing relations. Family: Emotional involvement, connection, supportive and quality time.

6. **Health**: Regular exercise, rest, healthy diet, weight control. Stress and time management, fun, rest and play.

7. **Having**: Meaningful and fulfilling time for creative expression and fulfillment.

8. **Profession**: Contented, fulfilled and using your abilities.

9. **Finances**: Living within means, responsible, saving and giving.

10. **Spirituality**: Commitment, active devotional, worship and active service to others.

> "Dream no small dreams. They have no power to stir the souls of men."
> Victor Hugo

9.7 FROM POVERTY TO REAL WEALTH

I define wealth as abundance in our life. For everyone that means something different. Wealth is about finding that point in your life where you have abundance. An **abundance** of **joy**, an abundance of **money**, an abundance of **time**, an abundance of **health** and an abundance of **God**. Most people spend their lives in trade offs. They find an abundance of money but trade their time at a job that doesn't inspire them. Some focus only on spending their time on what they want and suffer from a lack of money sufficient to share with others. As wise men say: "Balance is the key!" But what can we do to be wealthier, in the traditional sense of the word?

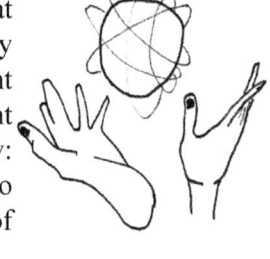

ATTRACT IT

1. Be a source of **positive vibration**. You will attract the same.

2. Forget yourself in a **service** you like for others.

3. Forgive, feel **gratitude** for everything, clear your mind of negative influences and have prosperity with God by your side.

CREATE IT

1. Know exactly what you want and "**go the extra mile.**"

2. Have an absolute **commitment** and love your work.

3. **Think big**. One idea could make me you a millionaire.

MANAGE IT

1. Create it, save it and invest it: **The mindset of the rich**.

2. Understand money as **seeds** to be planted and they will grow into money trees and understand the magic of compound interest.

3. Always have an **emergency fund** that covers your living expenses for six months. That will give you a lot of security.

SHARE IT

1. Celebrate by **giving** something back to society.

2. With **clear goals** and a focus on results, private wealth in the form of foundations can change the world.

3. **Help** with knowledge or resources to others less lucky than you.

"He who has injured thee was stronger or weaker than thee. If weaker, spare him; if stronger, spare thyself."
Seneca

9.8 FROM WEAKNESS TO STRENGTH

THOUGHTS

1. You have **control** over your life. If you think this is right or not, you are right, anyway! Think about wealth, not poverty.

2. Think in **learning** and growing. There is always something to learn and anyone can teach you a lesson, regardless of their position at work.

3. Make abundance your way of being, see **opportunities** everywhere. Save to make intelligent investments. Be proactive and solve problems. Think it, see it and it will happen.

FEELINGS

4. Think **big** and feel great about what you are going to create. You are going to create a better life for your clients, loved ones

and yourself!

    5. Feel whatever fear comes to your mind and **do your job** with firm resolution and commit to improving your life.

    6. You don't wish to be rich, **you are going to be rich** and can anticipate all the wonderful things that are going to happen. Use autosuggestions to reprogram your subconscious mind and give a percentage of your income to social causes with a glad spirit. Therefore, you will be increasing your attraction power (law of attraction) and decreasing the repelling tendency. According to this law, you repel what you are addicted to.

ACTIONS

    7. Play to **win**, not to avoid losing. Manage your money with financial intelligence. It is more important to manage well than to have high earnings. Benefit = income − outcome. Make your money work hard.

    8. Do a **brainstorming** exercise. List as many possibilities you can to start generating more income with active (promotion) as well as passive activities (writing a book, recording a cd, making a film).

    9. Make a list of ten of your favorite millionaires, study them, see what strategies they applied and start doing the same.

    10. Start being paid for results and not for time spent at work. Make a good financial plan for your life.

    "We've chosen the path to equality; don't let them turn us around."
    Geraldine Ferraro

9.9 FROM POOR TO RICH MENTALITY

I remember a cartoon I saw that illustrates the concept of mind awareness very well. There is this employee, Peter, who goes to his boss and says: "Dear Mr. Smith, I have worked in this company for the last 5 years, working really hard, I never got a raise, I think it is time to change that!" Mr. Smith looked at him and said: "Yes, dear Peter, but you know, the rich are getting richer, the poor poorer. A raise in your salary would mess things up!"

Start with your mind. Poor class mentality: I have no money so I have to work harder, I work overtime to get more money, I have to do all the chores myself, I have no time to even imagine a better life, I have less time and money every day, I am getting poorer and poorer, I am getting nowhere in my life. On the other hand, **rich class mentality**: Think like a millionaire, hire people to do the chores, gain free time to imagine a better life, make an action plan, take action, manifest money from thoughts and actions, hire more people to gain more free time, create massive wealth and keep getting richer with more free time. Besides, realize money is just an idea. Change your beliefs about what is possible.

Stop loving money. Spend money to get money (investment, training) and strive for freedom. Just imagine and feel the possibilities. How would you feel if you did not have to do the same repetitive activities you are doing today? How would you like to reach the point where you had no financial stress in your life anymore? Focus on what you want, not on what you don't want.

Do you want to produce miracles? Believe and take action. What would you do if you had all the money you ever wanted? You can do it now! Start your dream right now, if not when? Do you want to get rich quick? Provide value for as many people as you can, the quickest you can. Relax and say: "Everything is going to be okay!"

"While there's life, there's hope."
Marcus Tullius Cicero

9.10 FROM IGNORANCE TO RICHNESS

There is a science for getting rich. It is like algebra. If you only apply the laws that govern the processes of life, you will get the results you want. Remember, the main laws are perpetual transmutation, relativity, vibration, polarity, rhythm, cause and effect and gender. Let me leave you with some very important principles I learned in *"The Science of Getting Rich"* by **Wallace D. Wattles**.

You have the right to be rich. It is perfectly normal that you desire to be rich and the best we can do is to make the most out of ourselves. The concept of increasing Life is phenomenal, this is "**The Great Secret of Life:**" think it, feel it, do it and you will attract it. The intelligence substance, which is everywhere and lives in everything, lives in you. That which makes you want more money is the same that makes the plant grow. It is life, seeking fuller expression.

Gratitude! Believe that there is one intelligent substance from which all things proceed, believe this substance gives you everything you desire and feel a deep and profound gratitude for everything you are. You are an advancing person! No matter what your profession is, if you can give increase of life to others and make them sensible of this gift, they will be attracted to you, and you will get rich.

Take effective action. Start where you are. You can advance only by being larger than your present place. Act in a certain way. You must connect your positive thoughts with positive actions. Use the will to keep your mind fixed with faith and purpose on the vision of what you want and close your mind against all that may tend to shake your purpose.

"Hold the image of your dream, feeling the joy, take massive action and see the results you deserve in your life!"
Oscar Escallada

10. SPIRITUALITY
What type of spiritual relationship do you want to experience and how do you do it?

GODDESS MINERVA

Search for personal wisdom,

It is the quickest shortcut to happiness

Goddess of wisdom and spiritual experience

1. **How do you go from theory to practice?**

From lack of knowledge and practice to altruism and solidarity

2. **Do you want to include miracles in your daily ritual?**

From wanting to doing and from powerlessness to daily miracles

3. **What are the benefits for your health and humanity?**

From ignorance and cruelty to well-being and giving example

4. **Do you want to develop unconquerable strength?**

From fragility and wishing to strength and commitment

5. **Why should you become a spiritual giver!**

From taking and religion to giving and spirituality

10.1 FROM IGNORANCE TO THEORY

. How shall I start this section? I would like it to be as easy to read, as inspirational and as practical as possible. How could I communicate the vast knowledge of spirituality and religion to the reader and make it useful? Let us start by what we know.

Spirituality. What for? Since the very beginning of time, the human being has been looking for a paradise where happiness reigns. How? Through religion or wisdom, through faith or knowledge. I presume the best option is to use both. We search in spirituality to feel the connection with God, the Universe and the unknown forces. We look for certainty, control, security, support and strength to believe in ourselves and lead the lives we want, solve what we can control and be protected of the things we cannot control. On the other hand, we search for more knowledge to improve the many aspects of our life.

Religion is an organized and institutionalized way of experiencing spirituality. We normally believe "our religion" is the right one, even without knowing the rest. What do you know about your own religion? What about Buddhism or Hinduism, for example? My humble suggestion: learn more about different religions and practice the one that makes you a better person.

Hinduism: unity, karma and progress towards reincarnation.

Buddhism: Siddhartha, The Middle Way and reincarnation.

Islam: Muhammad, the Qur'an and the Hadith.

Confucianism: Confucius, individual morality and ethics.

Christianity: Christ, original sin and the Holy Trinity.

Judaism: Abraham, The Torah and the promised land.

Practice the law of thinking: Maintain a positive mental state, for it will regulate the action and direction of all your forces.

"The most dangerous creation of any society is the man who has nothing to lose." - **James Baldwin**

10.2 FROM THEORY TO PRACTICE

Does spirituality really make you happier? Scientific studies show that people who are either religious or spiritual or both are happier, face life's challenges in a more positive way and recover quicker from disease. There are two types of spirituality. One is religious faith. We have seen there are  many religions in the world. So the best advice is to choose the one that best nurtures your spirit. The second is spiritual awareness. The word spirit has many meanings, but in essence it is the non-physical part.

The world population is about 7 billion and it has been estimated that only about 1 billion people practice a religion regularly. That leaves almost 6 billion people without a religion. Therefore, the best option would be to develop the awareness and practice of spiritual values for humanity. Values of compassion, human warmth and affection for their health, happiness and peace of mind. Either way, religion, spirituality or both. I do believe spirituality makes you happier and I sincerely suggest the reader to learn more about how to experience spirituality on a daily basis. With what purpose? To be happier, to make those around you happier and to make this world a better place to live in. **Living by example is the greatest gift you can give!**

Let us see how you can **bring spirituality into your life**. Realize that we are surrounded by spirituality, it is in everyone and everywhere. We are all spiritual beings in physical bodies. Look at your loved ones, experience the love you feel for them. That love is pure joy and that's spirituality. Whatever makes you feel peaceful, joyful and content is spirituality. Notice and be part of all the acts of kindness you encounter throughout your day. Devote just a few minutes a day to quietly meditate on all the good things in your life, that's spirituality!

Practice the law of supply: As Jesus said: "What things so ever ye desire, when ye pray, believing and ye shall have them."

"Nothing is better for the body than the growth of the spirit."
Chinese Proverb

10.3 FROM WISHING TO DAILY ACTIONS

The Knight and the Wizard

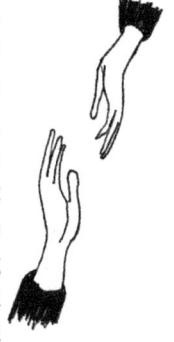

Once upon a time, there was this knight in the kingdom called "Success." The knight was very successful, he had everything anyone could hope for: spectacular health, wealth, a beautiful family, social recognition and enough time to enjoy all his achievements, but... there was just one thing that disturbed such a noble gentleman. He felt some kind of emptiness. One day, he was riding along the bank of the river lost in thought and a wizard from the kingdom of "Spirituality" called him and said: "Dear noble man, sorry to disturb but I see you look troubled, can I help?" The knight said: "My dear wizard, I have everything a man could wish for but I feel **emptiness** inside."

Then the wizard told him about how they lived in the kingdom of Spirituality. They considered **balance and spirituality** the most important things in life. People tried to have good health, the necessary means to live, save a bit for emergencies, enjoy their profession, love one another, have a home and family filled with love and enjoy various sports and leisure activities. People are full of love, live the spiritual values and feel connected to the universal intelligence and with one another.

The knight listened to him very carefully and was amazed, perhaps that was what he had been missing all these years! "How can I develop such spirituality, dear wizard?" the night asked. "Think, feel and behave every day following these principles: love unconditionally, forgive, learn solidarity and altruism, be generous, compassionate, understanding, kind and magnanimous. That emptiness will be filled with a growing and ever-expanding inner light that will make your life happier," the wizard replied.

Practice the law of attraction: Desire connects you with the thing desired and expectation draws it to your life. That is the Law.

"Happiness is not a destination. It is a method of life."
Burton Hills

10.4 FROM POWERLESSNESS TO DAILY MIRACLES

What is a miracle? There are many meanings. However, I have two personal definitions. First, you are surrounded by miracles (incredible things, happenings, phenomena) in your life. Realize that and you will regain the excitement of a child when he/she goes to a toy store for the first time (planes, nuclear energy, telepathy, television, telephone, generosity, lovers' reconciliation). Second, creating or achieving a result (an object, a goal) that was not thought possible before. **What can you do** to create your own miracle of happiness in your life?

THOUGHTS

1. Develop positive expectation and support it with action and **persistence**. Do not give up and you will achieve your "miracles."

2. Clear away self-limiting beliefs and take **full responsibility** for your thoughts, for your feelings and for your actions and results.

3. Focus your intent, do your work but release the how, **do not worry** too much, it will come to you, now it is in the hands of the universe.

FEELINGS

4. Trust your own inner guidance (inner voice, intuition, inspiration). **Expect** the miracles and let the universe figure out the details!

5. **Forgiveness** is essential. Forgive yourself first and then others.

6. **Gratitude**. What you focus on, expands, negative or positive.

ACTIONS

7. Make a list of **limiting beliefs** and get rid of them.

8. Create your **story of miracles** and send it to me to my mail address.

9. **A miracle a day.** Make a list of all miracles you see and want.

10. **Have fun**, be outrageous making a list of your own miracles; things, events, results you would love to have, produce or see in your life. Think you were born to be happy and to create the life you want. Remember, if you have the desire, you can attract it to your life! Go and start making plans and taking action!

Practice the law of receiving: You are to give your life, interest, energy and love, gratitude and it will come back to multiplied.

"**Above all, love each other deeply, because love covers over a multitude of sins.**"
The Bible, (1 Peter 4:8-9)

10.5 FROM SELFISHNESS TO SOCIAL RESPONSIBILITY

THE WORLD IN YEAR 2060

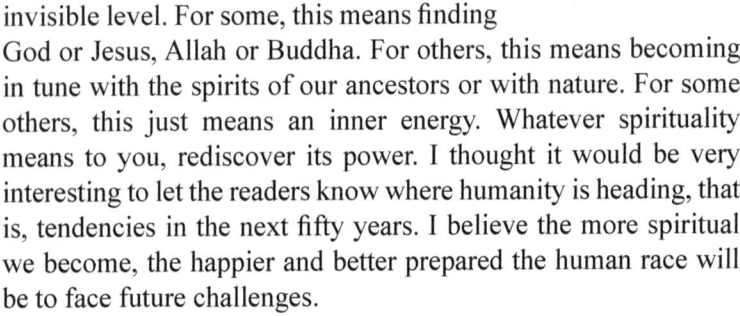

I think spirituality connects us all at an invisible level. For some, this means finding God or Jesus, Allah or Buddha. For others, this means becoming in tune with the spirits of our ancestors or with nature. For some others, this just means an inner energy. Whatever spirituality means to you, rediscover its power. I thought it would be very interesting to let the readers know where humanity is heading, that is, tendencies in the next fifty years. I believe the more spiritual we become, the happier and better prepared the human race will be to face future challenges.

1. **Thinking**: The human race will have to develop two traits, flexibility and adaptation capacity. There will be a population explosion (10 billion in year 2060) and a new technology era.

2. **Feeling**: Knowledge of happiness and emotions will be common for everybody, resulting in higher potential for happiness.

3. **Actions**: leadership is needed to face the new challenges.

4. **Individual being**: a new citizen with new abilities will emerge.

5. **Social being**: technology will improve various fields such as medicine, brain disease, robots, computers and world resources.

6. **Health**: diseases will be cured and life expectancy will grow.

7. **Having**: security will improve, higher access to information.

8. **Profession**: The environment industry will grow, employing millions of people.

9. **Finances**: The flow of capital and economic growth will

be less concentrated in the Western World. China and India will be the new economic leaders, probably with the same importance.

10. **Spirituality**: It remains a mystery but it is sure that the concept and experience of the spirit will evolve a great deal for the better, developing world conscience and unity between reason and faith.

Practice the law of increase: Take what you have and build upon it, with praise and gratitude and it will increase.

"**People do not lack strength, they lack will.**"
Victor Hugo

10.6 FROM IGNORANCE TO HAPPINESS WITH SPIRITUALITY

We cannot deny scientific proof any more that spirituality and religion have a positive effect on happiness, health and well-being. Only in the United States 95% of the population believe in God. My intention is not to convince anybody but to show that spirituality can add great value to our life. Let us see how we can lead happier lives with spirituality:

THOUGHTS

1. **Reflect** on inner and outer happiness. Research shows that 90% of happiness comes from inside, with only 10 percent derived from external things like a big house or a lot of money.

2. Find **your personal way** of spirituality. Center your life in God or in a higher reason like truth, love, inner happiness or enlightenment.

3. Live as a **philosopher of happiness**. You can go the fast way to enlightenment, Diogenes (live like a yogi), the middle way, Epicurus (live inner and outer happiness at the same time) or the way to unenlightenment like Aristippus (outer pleasure and inner suffering).

FEELINGS

4. Increase **self-esteem**. Learn new ideas, develop your own opinion.

5. Do activities that give you a sense of calm and **inner peace**.

6. Make a list of all **positive feelings** and experience them daily.

ACTIONS

7. Write your own journal where you can write the actions you take and how they affect your life and all life's experiences.

8. **Prayer**. Communicate with your higher self. Express gratitude, ask for forgiveness, strength and support for you and your loved ones.

9. **Start meditating**. Close your eyes, breathe in and out and repeat a short word like "one." Your mind is clear, you see thoughts come and go like clouds in the sky. Join a group if you need motivation at first.

10. Think about life, try out, find your way and realize your inner happiness. May we all find our path of **wisdom**, love and peace!

Practice the law of compensation: Your right place is where you can enjoy success. Excellent service equals excellent results.

"Only do what your heart tells you."
Princess Diana

10.7 FROM FRAGILITY TO STRENGTH IN HAPPINESS

I would like to illustrate the concept of personal strength and spirituality in this section. Some people do not believe or do not use the power of spirituality in their lives but I am a firm supporter of developing spiritual values in all areas. You may be able to do extraordinary things only with the power of your mind. However, how much more do you think you could **achieve with God by your side**? Let me share with you what gives me strength to become a better person every day and develop my spiritual side:

1. **Choice** is your in-born right. Focus your mind with the idea of providing the best possible service to humanity.

2. **Gratitude**. Be thankful for all you are. How much would you sell one of your eyes for? You are priceless.

3. **Ambition.** As a way of "gift" to your work and to the world.

4. **Personal improvement**. The more I develop my intellectual, emotional and practical abilities, the more I can contribute.

5. **Social responsibility**. Once you have control of your life, try to touch humanity with your actions. Help those who cannot help themselves, volunteer, play with children, talk to old people.

6. **Health**. The healthier I am, the more I can improve the rest of life's areas and the more I can contribute to others.

7. **Work**. Create your own balance of work and other areas and perform your work with passion and a sense of service to society.

8. **Money**. Enough possessions will help you feel security. However, once you meet those needs, extra amounts of money does not really add much to the feeling of happiness. Share it!

9. **Family and Partner.** Learn to love without conditions.

10. **Spirituality/religion.** Feel the connection and do good things.

Practice the law of non-resistance: Remove any obstacle by blessing and understanding it. Make it no longer a stumbling block, but a stepping stone, leading to your dream life.

**"There are two levers for moving men: interest and fear."
Napoleon Bonaparte**

10.8 FROM DOUBT TO SPIRITUALITY AT WORK

A monk asked his master: "What does Buddha mean?" The master replied: "the cypress tree in the garden. Let's imagine this cypress tree, spreading over the path in the monastery garden. What could be more ordinary, or familiar, than the aged tree that each monk passed every day for the whole of his life? In that sense, the cypress tree means the most familiar things." What familiar things do you pass by every day? Is it your home, your family, your work place, your coworkers? We can see in spirituality a way of life based on the premise of **awakening to a whole new perspective**, where numerous gifts are to be found if we only allow ourselves to enjoy them. I did and I can tell you, the satisfaction at work and at a personal level changed like night and day.

THOUGHTS

1. **Serenity** and peace of mind. Focus your mind on how you can become a better person in all areas of life, including work.

2. Have **faith** in all your abilities and your incredible potential.

3. Show **gratitude** and modesty among your peers.

FEELINGS

4. Give others the **gift of joy** and share your warmth with them.

5. Show **kindness**, compassion and mercy, according to situation.

6. **Help** people build up self-esteem and confidence.

ACTIONS

7. Let your actions be guided by humanity, **respect** and honesty.

8. Spend **time** with your co-workers and get to know them.

9. Change from taking to first giving. It is a whole new world!

10. Be magnanimous, humble, generous, gentle and strong before challenges. Become a **leader** by example.

Practice the law of sacrifice and obedience: Discipline is the road that leads to everything that makes life worth living. The closer you follow the laws, the more safety, prosperity and happiness you will have in all areas of your life.

"**I'm not afraid of storms, for I'm learning to sail my ship.**"
Louisa May Alcott

10.9 FROM UNBALANCE TO A BALANCED LIFE

The monk who sold his Ferrari by Robin S Sharma

This well crafted story by Robin S Sharma is the tale of Julian Mantle, a lawyer brought face to face with a spiritual crisis. Julian, he embarks on a life-changing odyssey and discovers the ancient culture of India. He had achieved everything most of us could ever want: professional success with a seven figure income, a grand mansion in a neighborhood inhabited by celebrities, a private jet, a summer home on a tropical island and his prized possession, a shiny red Ferrari parked in the center of his driveway. Suddenly, he has to come to terms with the unexpected effects of his unbalanced lifestyle. Let us see what we can **learn** from it?

THOUGHTS

During this journey he learns to value time as the most important commodity and how to cherish relationships, develop joyful thoughts and live fully, one day at a time. He tells us how to cultivate the mind, find the lesson in setbacks and follow our own purpose. As we see, we should see the pursuit of wealth as one more of life's goals and share it with others as much as we can.

FEELINGS

We learn to view wealth in terms of inner peace and joy. It also makes us aware of the so-called rat race for material success and money, and the potential danger of forgetting the rest of areas.

ACTIONS

Julian was miraculously transformed into a healthy man with physical vitality and spiritual strength. He learned the virtue of selflessness in serving others, never to sacrifice happiness for achievements, to enjoy the journey of life, to live each day as his last and to spread these secrets for the benefit of other people.

Practice the law of forgiveness: Only as we forgive are we forgiven. Forgive and you shall be free of negative emotions and a prosperous consciousness shall abound.

"An honest heart possesses a kingdom."
Seneca

10.10 FROM IGNORANCE TO THE WISDOM OF HAPPINESS

"THE LIVING RANGE"

We have come a long way! In this final chapter I wanted to give the reader a special gift. I wanted to summarize my own wisdom about happiness and how I apply it to my own life. It is actually a principle for life, I call it the "The Living Range."

It has two parts. **First**, develop the ability of being happy for no reason, you were born happy! Being happy is a general feeling that is with you all your life. Good and bad things will happen to you and they will probably create positive and negative emotions, but they are just temporary. **Second**, in all areas of life there are acceptable minimums and maximums to hope for. What I do is define my acceptable minimum and have a strategy for the **worst possible scenario**. That is my basis, my home, my security (first human need). I build from there, I dream from there and I give my best to reach my goals and become a happier person, as I am a happy-born individual. As they say: "Everything can be improved." Let me show you:

1. **Thinking**: from clarity of thought to wisdom in all areas.

2. **Feeling**: from feeling happy to being happy all the time.

3. **Actions**: from discipline to excellence.

4. **Individual** being: from being average to doing your best.

5. **Social** being: from a member of society to social leader.

6. **Health**: form average to spectacular.

7. **Having**: from the minimum to the maximum.

8. **Profession**: from self-realization to social wealth creator.

9. **Finances**: from emergency plan to financial independence.

10. **Spirituality**: from awareness to constant living.

Practice the law of success: You were born to be rich and happy. You can if you think you can. Infinite resources are at your disposal. Why don't you make use of them?

"Being happy is simple. Allow yourself to be happy and take little steps every day to be a bit happier in all areas."
Oscar Escallada

You Were Born Happy!

THIRD PART THE PRACTICE OF HAPPINESS

1. DAILY PRACTICE

Dear reader, how was your experience through the mountains and valleys of life? We started with **Jupiter** and the mind, then **Juno** and the emotions; after that, **Neptune** and the world of action; then followed the God **Vulcan** to assist us in building our chosen best self; and at the end, the Goddess **Vesta** and her incredible powers to help us improve our relationships in all areas. That was the **first half** of our journey.

In the **second half**, we started with the Goddess of health, **Hygeia**, who will help us transform our bodies and develop healthy habits. Next, we encountered **Pluto**, the God of riches and good fortune. He will lead the path to find our own wealth. After that, we met the incredible **Mercury**, God of trade, profit and commerce. With him we learnt that God gave us more talent and ability than we could possibly imagine, we just have to use it and return the gift to God. We then entered the kingdom of finances and we learnt from the Goddess **Abundia** that the first thing we should do is finding our purpose in life and then riches will naturally follow. Finally, we met **Minerva**, Goddess of wisdom and spiritual experience. She taught us that we are spiritual beings in physical bodies, how to live spirituality in our daily lives and how to find wisdom.

Now, the most interesting part of the quest starts. All the positive ideas and emotions we have experienced on the way, all the wonderful dreams we have envisioned and all the good actions we have wished we would have taken should be integrated in your life **on a daily basis** through a properly organized plan. Furthermore, I believe now you have two options. First, you do the 100-day program, where you work with one value each day. Second, you choose the values that appeal most to you for as long as you want.

The idea is to help readers apply all concepts to their daily lives.

100 VALUES – 100 DAYS PROGRAM

I strongly encourage you to organize your happiness plan this way. It means you work on one value everyday for the next 100 days. I promise you, at the end of the program you will be another person. Your level and awareness of happiness will have changed so much that you will be asking yourself why you had not done it before.

I encourage you to set a **date** to start with the program. Before you start, reread the book again and think about what you would like to accomplish in each of the chapters. With that in mind, read one chapter a day. Write in your Happiness **diary**, the **actions** you are going to take to integrate that change in your life. You do that every single day for the rest 100 days and your life will never be the same again.

This option is a general conception, where you produce small changes in all areas of life, resulting in an extraordinary change, a **quantum leap** in the quality of your life.

A LA CARTE PROGRAM

This is the second option. "A la carte" is a French expression, meaning, according to **your choice**. Here you choose the values you want to concentrate on, the number of actions you want to take per value and the amount of time you want to work on a certain value.

This is a better program if you are particularly interested in developing just one area or a specific number of values in the different areas of life. There might be some people who are only interested in working on a certain value or area. Here, you can also experience a quantum leap as a result of small daily changes. This is like the experiment of **changing a glass of water** colored in red and you start adding drops of normal water. At the end the red water becomes transparent.

FROM \ TO		WINNER'S IMAGE / LOW SELF-ESTEEM	CONFIDENCE / LOW CONFIDENCE	CLARITY / CONFUSION	DECISION / INDECISION	COMMITMENT / INDIFFERENCE
THOUGHTS	1	who do you want to be?	take inventory	change potential awareness	the power of your mind	infinite supply
THOUGHTS	2	make a commitment	be caring	forget past failure	be true to yourself	you can reach any goal
THOUGHTS	3	hold the image in your mind	stay in the moment	focus on future success	5 senses and 6 mental faculties	unlimited creativity
FEELINGS	1	relax	celebrate your journey	learn form dissatisfaction	continous happiness	passion & relief
FEELINGS	2	create positive feelings	know you will reach your goals	feel happy	use subconscious mind	create your emotions
FEELINGS	3	be responsible for everything	feel joy of sharing	chooose your heart's desire	use reason	live with passion
ACTIONS	1	create a dream board	do what you love	from wish to must	3 top goals	take massive action
ACTIONS	2	have role models	heolp others	visualize	follow your feelings	binding commitment
ACTIONS	3	make necessary changes	improve yourself	be flexible	decision check	make & follow your plan
ACTIONS	4	share your knowledge	be proactive	be creative	make your motto	review your progress

FROM \ TO		BELIEF / LACK OF FAITH	ENTHUSIASM / BOREDOM	EFFICIENCY / INEFFICIENCY	RESULTS / LOW ACHIEVEMENT	WISDOM-LAWS / IGNORANCE
THOUGHTS	1	remove mental blocks	choose meaning of reality	think of extraordinary results	ONE DREAM	perpetual transmutation
	2	find your worthy goal	share your gift	I CAN	determination	relativity
	3	follow your dream	be authentic	team work	pesistence	thinking
FEELINGS	1	expect your desire	learn lessons in problems	feel the fear & do it!	take care of your security	vibration & atrraction
	2	accept only the positive	feel postive emotions	go through the terror barrier	be flexible	relativity
	3	destroy doubt with faith	celebrate the joy of life	be proud of your success	positive attitude	compensation
ACTIONS	1	create a vacuum	do your affirmations	6 actions to make the difference	redifine goals as you go	polarity
	2	make goal cards	do what you love	use Pareto 20% - 80%	reward yourself	gender
	3	be an inspiration	increase strengths	own code of excellence	be accountable	cause & effect
	4	be your best	keep the flame burning	plan your time	find support	success

This is just an example of the first chapter, THINKING.
I invite you to download the rest of chapters for free
on my website:
www.happyglobe-oe.com

2. THE POWER OF YOUR MIND

We have an amazing power in our minds, we just have to learn to use it. According to scientific studies, the mind is divided in two parts, the conscious and the subconscious mind. On the one hand, the conscious mind works with the information coming from our senses like see, hear, smell, taste and touch. On the other hand, the subconscious mind is the emotional mind. It cannot differentiate between what is real and what is imagined.

How can we use both minds to lead a happier life?

CONSCIOUS MIND

Thinking is our highest function. Besides, we have been given the gift of higher mental faculties: Perception, Will, Imagination, Memory, Reason and Intuition. It is our responsibility to learn how to utilize and develop them to a higher degree.

The point here is not to be limited to what our 5 senses tell us, but to develop those 6 intellectual faculties to lead the life we want. **Perception**: we saw it all depends on your focus. **Will** is your ability to concentrate. **Imagination** creates fantasies, which you can turn into reality. **Memory** is perfect, you just have to exercise and develop it. **Reason** gives you the ability to think. **Finally**, Intuition is the ability to pick up vibrations all around you.

SUBCONCIOUS MIND

We spoke earlier about the **genie** of Aladdin's lamp. That gene is within us and it is called the subconscious mind. The truth is that you can accomplish anything you set your mind to, you just have to believe in yourself, otherwise it will not happen. Tell your subconscious mind what you want, see yourself doing and being that person, do your visualization and affirmation exercises with a lot of emotion twice a day and your belief in yourself will grow. This new belief in yourself will cause you to take actions you did not dare before and the results in your life will change like night and day. Believe me, I have experienced the transition in my own life. **This is the great secret to happiness and fulfillment.**

3. EMOTIONAL & SOCIAL INTELLIGENCE

Two of the most important skills you can develop to be a more happy individual and as a happy member of any group, family, friends and work, is to develop not only emotional but also social intelligence.

Let us have a look at how we can develop intelligence in both fields:

THOUGHTS

1. **Know yourself.** Recognize your emotions. Learn to differentiate between emotions and the reason behind them and what you can do to increase the positive and channel the negative ones.

2. **Read others.** Be aware of the emotions of others, appreciate them and understand how and why people feel the way they do.

3. **Perceive accurately.** Be as objective as you can when you assess a situation, the people involved and its outcome.

FEELINGS

4. **Resist** or delay any impulse. When we become skilled at sensing, labeling, and using our own emotions, we are able to harness them as a source of information and motivation.

5. **Control** aggression, hostility or irresponsible behavior. Control the expression of your negative emotions but learn to know why you feel that way. There is very valuable information in your experience.

6. **Manage emotions** in a flexible and adaptable way. You want to develop positive and constructive relations with others.

ACTIONS

7. **Be authentic.** Nobody likes people who are not real. Be true to yourself, remember "Time puts everybody in his/her place."

8. **Address your needs** as well as the need of others. First, know what you need and want and then be conscious that other people also have their own needs and desires.

9. **Choose yourself.** Become your own expert in self-management. Focus on consciously choosing your thoughts, feelings and actions.

10. **Give yourself.** It means developing self-direction. It comes from using empathy and principled decision-making to increase wisdom and create a more compassionate, healthy world.

"And be ye kind one to another, tender-hearted, forgiving one another, even as God for Christ's sake hath forgiven you."
Ephesians 4:32

4. HOW CAN I BE HAPPIER? A SUMMARY

Let us make a summary of everything we learned:

1. **Do your morning and evening rituals**: relax, learn to enjoy the very moment you experience, be grateful for all the things you have, focus on your dreams and send good wishes to humanity.

2. **Change your mental focus**. You now have 1,000 thoughts, feelings and actions you can apply immediately to your life. You can change from the negative to the positive side of the 100 human values we have covered.

3. **Lead by example**. Make the commitment with yourself of being an example of happy living for others to follow. Remember to keep the lessons of the past, live the present to the fullest and hope for better things in the future, taking massive action.

4. **Come to terms with your own existence**, get clear about what is important to you and help others along the way.

MIND

You are free to use the unlimited power of your mind

FEELINGS

Love yourself, your fellowmen and women and life

ACTIONS

Be responsible for the results of your actions

INDIVIDUAL BEING

Your best tools are sense of humor and optimism

Be courageous to lead the life of your dreams

SOCIAL BEING

Understanding and open communication are the best ways to interact with the world around you

BODY

Treat your body as you would like it to treat you

POSSESSIONS

Enjoy anything and everything

PROFESSION

Find purpose in what you do

FINANCES

Create multiple sources of passive income

SPIRITUALITY

Let wisdom, common sense and curiosity lead your way

5. START CREATING MIRACLES IN YOUR LIFE!

Let us call them "your life' miracles." I encourage you to take your life to the next level.

MIND

Know what you want and persists until you achieve it

FEELINGS

Let love be the ruling principle of your life

ACTIONS

Take massive action, review progress and be flexible

INDIVIDUAL BEING

Be the person you have always wanted to be

SOCIAL BEING

Become the person you have always longed for

BODY

Have the spectacular body and vitality you deserve

POSSESSIONS

Plan, have and enjoy everything you desire

PROFESSION

Be the professional you want to be

FINANCES

Make a plan to become financially independent and follow it

SPIRITUALITY

Let the spiritual side come alive and guide you

"You choose your life, thoughts, feelings and actions."
Oscar Escallada

CONCLUSION

LEADING AN EXTRAORDINARY LIFE

You can lead a passionate life, only if you think you can. See life as a constant and marvelous experience and enjoy the process as much as the goal. Combine youth´s spontaneity with the wisdom of experience to continue growing, learning and loving.

Live every single day as if it were the most important day of your whole life, in fact it is. Our final destiny is the result of our apparently little decisions we take every day.

If you control your thoughts, feelings and actions, you will be controlling your own destiny, without regard for external circumstances. The most important aspect you should control is your inner world. We all have the power of giving meaning to everything outside ourselves.

The only limits you have are self imposed in your imagination. Overcoming difficulties shapes your character and creates your personality.

Anyone of us has the potential of becoming the hero of his life, when we make decisions with courage, even in most difficult situations. Winners in life defy adversity, doing what they think is correct in spite of external situations they face. Being a hero does not require an epic effort; small daily steps make a big difference.

Be ready to feel uncomfortable when you try new ideas or actions. You are out of your comfort zone and that means you are growing. You should be ready to take the blows and keep moving forward; otherwise, you will never know the limits of what you are able to accomplish.

Contribution to society is not an obligation, it is an opportunity to give back some of your blessings and make the world a better place for all. Try making small actions to help others. This is the surest way of developing a noble and powerful personality.

You Were Born Happy!

CREATE THE LIFE OF YOUR DREAMS

These are the questions leading to your treasures:

1. What kind of thinking do you want to have?
2. What feelings do you long for?
3. What actions do you want to take?
4. Who do you want to be?
5. What social relations would you love to develop?
6. What physical body and wellbeing would you love?
7. What are your dream possessions (cars, houses…)?
8. What is your dream profession?
9. How much money do you want?
10. What kind of spiritual existence do you desire?

And these are the 10 treasures the gods gave us:

1. Choose your thoughts and you choose your life.
2. Let love be your guidance in all situations.
3. You will accomplish anything with persistence.
4. Act as the person you want to become.
5. Always be of service to your fellowmen.
6. Treat your body as you would like it to treat you.
7. Quality service to society is the key to wealth.
8. Be the best you can be, that is the greatest gift.
9. Find your life's purpose, the money will follow.
10. Look for wisdom, happiness will appear.

REACHING THE SUMMIT

THE SEARCH CONTINUES…

Congratulations dear reader!

You made it! You went through all the ten valleys, got to know the gods and goddesses, got acquainted with the genie inside of you and discovered the secrets of real, happy living. However, this is just the beginning of your new life. What you do with these secrets is your responsibility. I encourage you to use them every day of your life and help as many people as you can in this adventure called life. The more people we are, the better will be for the whole of humanity and the human race.

God bless you.

ABOUT THE AUTHOR

I was born and raised in a beautiful city in the North of Spain called Santander. From a very early age I was absolutely passionate about understanding human nature and helping those around me as much as I could.

My life is a living example of constant achievement. At age 17, I left my home country to discover the world, worked and studied in USA, Canada, United Kingdom, Germany, France, Mexico and Cuba. Throughout the years I completed two degrees (psychology and languages), three master´s degrees (hotel management, human resources and finances/marketing) and became proficient in four languages. I have always striven to be my best in all professional positions (teacher, translator, salesman and hotel manager), constantly "going the extra mile."

Today, I have the honor and satisfaction of working with Bob Proctor, teaching worldwide proven Life Success Strategies and helping people become healthier, wealthier and happier.

What is your deepest heart´s desire? Are you living the life of your dreams?

Let me take you by the hand, walk with you every step of the way and make phenomenal changes in your life, whatever it takes. I believe in the incredible greatness of your mind. Let me help you unleash all your potential with passion and purpose, with a constant focus on your desires and with the unstoppable force of complete determination. You cannot afford being less than you could be. Make your life an incredible adventure!

Matthew 7:7 "Ask and it will be given to you; seek and you will find; knock and the door will be opened to you."

HAPPY GLOBE

I created the website called Happy Globe for you and all those who are interested in learning how to be a bit happier every day. You can find products (books, cds, dvds, videos, articles), services (seminars, presentations, coaching, mastermind groups), the blog on happiness and many more surprises.

I invite you to visit the page at this address:

www.happyglobe-oe.com

Let me share with you a dream I have had on several occasions. I imagine the planet earth has a heart, beating every second. I imagine for every pulse there are two or more people gathering to speak about improving their level of happiness. It is an interaction where someone teaches someone else a better way to improve a certain aspect of happiness. Furthermore, it is an interaction where the teacher becomes the student and the student becomes the teacher.

For more information on how you can become part of this extraordinary movement and community, contact us on the website.

**Additional Programs
and Products
to Help You Realize
Your Potential...**

"Somebody should tell us, right at the start of our lives, that we are dying. Then we might live life to the limit, every minute of every day. Do it! I say. Whatever you want to do, do it now! There are only so many tomorrows."
Michael Landon

THE HAPPINESS COACHING PROGRAM
YOU WERE BORN HAPPY

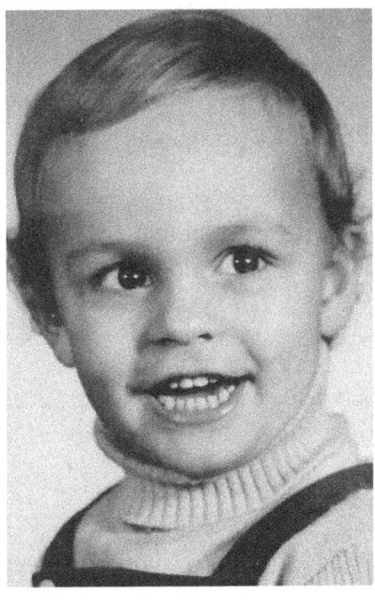

"Change your mental focus and you change your life."

Oscar Escallada

You can change your level of happiness in an instant. I changed my life and so can you. Let us work together.

A coach or mentor helps you transform your dreams into action, creating the necessary goal plan and then providing you with the information and resources you need to change your happiness awareness to the next level.

The power of coaching is based on the most critical ingredients for happiness: ongoing support, detailed action plans, constructive feedback and personal accountability.

The Oscar Escallada Happiness Coaching Program will show you the way to increase your awareness and level of happiness to a degree you never thought was possible. First, you will realize that being happy is a mental inner state. Then, you will begin to feel grateful for the joy of living. Finally, you will focus your mind, heart and actions on the positive side of 100 human values in the 10 most important areas of your life.

Visit: www.happyglobe-oe.com

Or email: o1escallada@hotmail.com

oscarescallada@lifesuccessconsultants.com

LIFE SUCCESS CONSULTANT

I became a LifeSuccess consultant in 2011 with Bob Proctor, the legend of the film "The Secret." I received the certification on April 1, 2011, authorizing me to coach and give seminar presentations on the following LifeSuccess Productions programs:

1. **You Were Born Rich**
You can unlock the hidden and rich potential that allows you to achieve every financial, emotional, physical and spiritual dream you've imagined for yourself.

2. **Goal Achiever**
There's a big difference between goal setting and goal achieving. We teach how to bridge that gap in this powerful program.

3. **Mission in Commission**
This program is particularly design for those of you who want to become sales experts and increase your earnings exponentially.

4. **Success Puzzle**
Sometimes, putting your life together is like trying to put a puzzle together without the cover picture on the puzzle box. How are you supposed to know how to build without a guide to help you?

5. **The Winner's Image**
The Winner's Image Program is a strong action-oriented program with powerful emphasis on accountability. Without THIS change, nothing else will change in your life!

You can contact me here:
www.oscarescallada.lisuccessconsultants.com
oscarescallada@lifesuccessconsultants.com

**"Tell me what you want and I will show you how to get it!"
Bob Proctor**

THINKING INTO RESULTS FACILITATOR

Another wonderful program I am also working on is **Thinking Into Results**. It is based on fifty years of Bob Proctor's internationally acclaimed teachings on the power of the mind.

LifeSuccess Corporate teaches business leaders at all levels how to unleash the potential of their most important asset—**their people.**

Many companies in this weakened economy are fighting the same battles with some barely surviving: resources spread too thin, sales slumping and unmotivated employees fearing the loss of their jobs. LifeSuccess' Corporate breakthrough programs provide the specific tools.

Thinking into Results is an extraordinary program that presents twelve logical, straightforward and practical lessons that ensure a thriving, success-driven company culture that translates into an exceptional return on investment for any company.

You Were Born Happy!

FOUNDATION THE GLORIOUS BEING CENTRE

GHANA, AFRICA

EMPOWERING
Children and Women to Greatness

Dear Reader,

When you buy this book, you will be supporting the Glorious Being Center in Ghana, Africa. A part of the benefits of this book support this marvelous project.

Glorious Being Center is a not-for-profit organization founded in 2004 dedicated to "Empowering Children and Women to Greatness." Its mission is to provide solutions to help the children of the world rise from poverty by providing safe and sustainable housing and food, along with a program of education:

(I) **Outer Building**: To provide safe and sanitary living conditions that include sustainable food supplies using the "permaculture" design system – you can read about it at www.gbcenter.org.

(II) **Inner Building**: A system that provides the children an empowering educational curriculum that creates a winning and positive mentality. This will enable them to develop their full potential and realize a better future.

Let me share with you a wonderful message by its president, Mrs. Gloria Ramirez: **"Each moment is magical, and when we embrace it as it comes, we ride the wave of happiness and inner peace."**

www.ingramcontent.com/pod-product-compliance
Lightning Source LLC
Chambersburg PA
CBHW061257110426
42742CB00012BA/1948